The Last Eve

Innocence Restored

The Last Eve
Innocence Restored

By
Kathy S. Gray

The Last Eve: Innocence Restored

Published by World Revival Press
9900 View High Drive
Kansas City, Missouri 64134

ISBN 1-58047- 007-6

For Worldwide Distribution

Printed in the United States of America

First Printing, May 2002

Cover Design by Randall Keeler
www.keelerinteractive.com

Typography/layout by Buck Sommerkamp

For other exciting releases from World Revival Press,
call (877) 804-5433.

This book is affectionately dedicated to:

Brooke-Linn Kay Pebworth
&
Allyson Grace King

I would like to personally acknowledge J.D. King and Joel Kilpatrick for their valued assistance in the formation and development of this book. Without their labor, this project would have never reached completion.

*"But I am afraid that just as Eve was deceived by
the serpent's cunning, your minds may somehow be
led astray from your sincere and pure devotion to
Christ."*

2 Corinthians 11:3

Table of Contents

Publisher's Preface

"Kathy's message…is a masterpiece…not for what she said, but how she said it. She preached not only with her mouth, but with her whole being, in demonstration of the truth…Many could preach the words she used, but few could deliver the words in the Spirit she delivered them." [1]

For over six years Kathy Gray has been at the forefront of the international revival movement. Her name has often been associated with the reemergence of spirit-empowered ministry. Through conferences, writing and weekly ministry at World Revival Church in Kansas City, Kathy Gray is igniting hearts for the Kingdom of God.

Numerous phrases have been used to describe Kathy and her ministry — some of which include: "powerful," "prophetic," "gut-wrenching." Perhaps none of these accurately convey the totality of what God is doing through her ministry. Kathy is a teacher, prayer warrior and model to hundreds of pastors' wives. After observing her ministry, a student from North Central Bible College in Minneapolis, Minnesota wrote, "Kathy has a powerful anointing of God's presence on her life and Pastor Gray lets her flow in it. It is about time! If we want to see revival go through the land, we need to let all of God's chosen workers do their job."[2]

World Revival Press is proud to announce the release of Kathy Gray's first major publication: *The Last Eve: Innocence Restored.* This book confronts the unsettling reality of the loss of innocence; giving insight into God's glorious plan of restoration. *The Last Eve* carefully walks us through the horrors of sin, challenging us to move into a place of victorious living.

Virtually every page of *The Last Eve* is filled with relevant Biblical teaching and practical application. In fact, at the conclusion of every chapter, reflection is made available through the inclusion of "application questions." These questions can either be utilized for group discussion or private reflection.

In a troubled world of confusing messages, *The Last Eve* was written to pierce hearts with the truth of Jesus Christ. We hope your heart is stirred and your spirit is ignited as the wonderful story of the Last Eve is depicted. For we are living in an hour when the Bride is being awakened to her glorious destiny.

When all is said and done, we will discover Kathy Gray is like the young woman who ignited the Welsh Revival of 1904 with the following words, "*If no one else will, then I must say that I love the Lord Jesus with all my heart."*[3]

Foreword

"…a man will…be united to his wife, and they will become one flesh." Genesis 2:24b

My wife Kathy has never been the traditional "pastor's wife," applauding and watching from the front row. Just as the Lord anointed me to serve in ministry, Kathy also has the calling of the Lord on her life. Over the years I have endeavored to find ways we could serve together. I believe teamwork has multiplied our ministerial impact several times over.

I have been astounded with the giftings Kathy's life has been graced with. Over the years she has become a capable administrator, teacher, as well as one who moves in the prophetic. Kathy has also shown herself to be a powerful preacher and talented musician.

I want you to know that Kathy is a woman whose life has been awakened in the presence of God. She has known trouble, but she has also known the grace of God. She journeyed through darkness, but has stepped into the glorious light. She is woman ignited by the fire of revival.

Just as Kathy was changed in the presence of God, this book was written that you might also experience transformation. As you read the following pages, carefully consider each and every word. Allow the stories and teaching to touch your Spirit. In the quiet of your reading, ask the Lord to reveal His heart to you. When all is said and done, apply the truth to your life.

I pray the Lord will bless you and make His face shine upon you.

-Steve Gray

Introduction

"I want you to be... innocent about what is evil."
Romans 16:19

Nothing compares to the feeling of walking into a newly decorated nursery. On a pink background, paintings of fluffy ducklings hang. Stacks of brand new blankets cover the awaiting crib. The corner holds a rocking chair and a changing table outfitted with towels and diapers. Teddy bears and stuffed animals line shelves along with pictures of mommy and daddy. The nursery feels inviting and secure. Like a nice warm hug, it exudes warmth and tenderness. When the infant closes her eyes in this environment, she is away from the world and all its evil.

Many of us try to recapture childhood innocence. We might reminisce about trimming the Christmas tree or sitting on grandpa's lap. Some hold on to the memory of a special moment, while others remember a perfectly ordinary day when things felt right. People save "snapshots" of childhood innocence; flipping through them like images in a photo album. These portraits represent a time when evil seemed nonexistent.

I vividly remember my daddy coming in every night and praying for me before I went to sleep. It would be difficult to describe the loving way he said, *"Kathy, you are God's little girl! You are going to have a great life!"* There in the safety of my father's affection, there were no worries, no fears. The pleasant memories of being with my father have stuck with me for years; summing up the very idea of innocence. I have found that innocence is a quiet place to which everyone longs to return.

A Revival of innocence

My husband Steve and I gave twelve years of our lives to a small-town church in the middle of America. In the midst of seemingly endless labor, we finally saw it grow to become a solid, healthy congregation. Innocence and simplicity rested upon the people and remained so for about the first eleven years. Yet things were about to change.

February and March of 1996, were two of the most difficult months in my life. One of the members of our congregation wrote in his journal, *"I believe that this is a widespread attack."* [4] Despite the fact that we had been praying together as a congregation for two and half years, there were a handful of people growing discontent. Amidst grumbling and threats, a few left our church plotting to destroy the work of God. Things became difficult. Soon we were in a tremendous battle for our marriage, our ministry and even our very lives. Our family lived under a constant barrage of the devil's flaming darts.

Soon my husband's discouragement was bordering on depression. All hope seemed gone. Steve talked about leaving the ministry and disappearing into some faraway jungle. Not knowing what else to do, I encouraged him to visit the revival at Brownsville Assembly of God in Pensacola, Florida.

While he was gone I began to do my best to lead the congregation, in spite of the raging battle. God helped me to preach anointed messages and lead worship, even while my heart was breaking. I encouraged the people the best I could, but there was heaviness resting on the entire congregation. Our innocence was being stolen. Randy Lohman described it well when he recounted the following,

> *"It was darkness. It was a time of night...I can remember all our men lying on the floor crying. We didn't know why we were crying. We just knew it was night...Our whole life was gone. I mean we were dead. We were covered with a thick blanket of death. There was no life. There was no movement of God...."* [5]

I began to wonder if our congregation would ever regain the innocence it once possessed?

On the rainy evening of March 24, 1996 everything changed. At 6:12 P.M. my husband returned from Pensacola, Florida and the power of God struck our entire congregation. One young girl in our church describes what happened:

> *"We all raced up to the front, shoes were flying everywhere, as people began jumping and dancing. Never in my life had I seen such a sight. I looked at pastor. He was just standing there with this look of shock on his face. Then he started jumping and twirling around with this silly grin on his face. I had never seen him look so happy."* [6]

In a split second of time, my husband's innocence was restored. The power of God did for us what we could not do on our own. Burdens were lifted and hurts were healed. When my husband was finally able to speak, he said, *"I don't know what this is, but I'm coming back tomorrow night to find out."* The next evening the entire congregation showed up!

Little did we know that we were about to enter into a historic outpouring of the Holy Spirit. Since that evening, visitors from fifty states and seventy nations visited our church. *Charisma* and other media sources have estimated over a quarter of million people have participated in the revival services in our congregation.

While great signs and wonders are being experienced in the revival, everything points back to the restoration

of innocence. Lives are being transformed and
slumbering hearts are being awakened. This revival
is helping us become what Jesus wanted when He
declared, *"…unless you change and become like little
children, you will never enter the kingdom of heaven."
Matthew 18:3b.* God is revealing innocence that:

- Removes layers of self-reliance

- Returns us to a childlike attitude

- Recreates us to accomplish His purposes

- Restores devotion to Jesus

Do you want to break away from things that steal your
innocence? This book will help you find your way back
to the innocence found in the Garden of Eden. Let's
take this life-transforming journey together, reaching
back to the innocence of the first woman and man,
and reaching forward to our destiny in Christ.

Kathy Gray
Kansas City, Missouri

Chapter One

What Ever Happened to Eve?

"Our failing is dreadful, our falling is shameful, and our dying is sorrowful."

— *Julian of Norwich (1342-1413)*

"WHEN THE WOMAN SAW THAT THE FRUIT OF
THE TREE WAS GOOD FOR FOOD AND PLEASING
TO THE EYE, AND ALSO DESIRABLE FOR GAINING
WISDOM, SHE TOOK SOME AND ATE IT. SHE
ALSO GAVE SOME TO HER HUSBAND, WHO WAS
WITH HER, AND HE ATE IT. THEN THE EYES
OF BOTH OF THEM WERE OPENED, AND THEY
REALIZED THEY WERE NAKED; SO THEY SEWED FIG
LEAVES TOGETHER AND MADE COVERINGS FOR
THEMSELVES." GENESIS 3:6-7

Thousands of years ago in a fragrant garden a woman walked in the glory of God. She had not only great beauty, but a wondrous disposition. This woman and her husband were truly the embodiment of all God desired in humanity. In innocence and simplicity they walked hand and hand with God.

Imagine the joy of fellowship afforded Eve and her husband. They beheld the wonder of encountering their Creator face-to-face! The intimacy they had with Him was greater than any couple this side of heaven. Their relationship was the most sacred of relationships.

The hand of God provided for every need Eve and her husband encountered. From virtually every direction, the garden was bursting with abundant provision. Eve could live her life without the slightest fear or need.

Evil seductively whispered into the ear of innocence, "Did God really say?" All became lost as Eve questioned the very character of God. She sank her teeth into the forbidden fruit and brought forth the corruption of humanity.

What ever happened to Eve?

Eve Hid Her Bareness

"Then the eyes of both of them were opened and they realized they were naked; so they sewed fig leaves together and made coverings for themselves." Genesis 3:7

In the beginning of time a woman stood "naked and unashamed." Possessing an unparalleled honesty and openness, she viewed the world through eyes of purity. As she journeyed through the fragrant garden, she possessed untainted life. In every way innocence was embodied.

Whatever happened to Eve?

As sin entered the picture, Eve took on a new disposition. A woman who formerly lived without pretense or guile now found herself hiding in the shadows. Gripped by her own iniquities, Eve covered herself. A life that once lived with openness and sincerity was now veiled.

Whatever happened to Eve?

God never intended for Eve to hide behind hastily constructed coverings. He wanted her life to be transparent and exposed. Do you live life with openness and authenticity or do you hide behind fig leaves of your own making?

Eve Brought Betrayal

"But the LORD God called… 'Where are you?'"
Genesis 3:9

In the Bible the Lord reveals Himself as a benevolent creator and faithful Father. He is often depicted as a God of compassion who sacrificially involves Himself in the affairs of His creation. The Lord is always patient, longsuffering and slow to anger. The goodness of God is unequaled throughout time and eternity.

Consequently Eve's betrayal is the most unsettling event in this tragedy. She betrayed the gracious and benevolent Father of creation. Choosing the deception of evil over the goodness of God, her loyalty was misplaced.

Whatever happened to Eve?

Eve and her husband were not ignorant. They knew what God expected. In the beginning the Lord declared His expectations to Eve and her husband in clarifying detail. He declared, *"You are free to eat from any tree in the garden; but you must not eat from the tree of the knowledge of good and evil, for when you eat of it you will surely die"* Genesis 2:16b-17. Rather than obey the command of the Lord, Eve and her husband embraced the pleasures of sin.

Whatever happened to Eve?

The moment teeth pierced the skin of the forbidden fruit, Eve and her husband denounced God. Their actions declared, "God, we question Your Word. We question Your character. We question Your motives." Consider what an insult this was to the Heavenly Father.

What ever happened to Eve?

The loss of innocence birthed betrayal in the hearts of humanity. Have you inherited from Eve a twisted human wisdom that elevates itself over the wisdom of God? Have you, like Eve, betrayed the Lord and those in positions of authority?

Eve was Barren

*"I will greatly increase your pains in childbearing;
with pain you will give birth to children."*
Genesis 3:16b

Eve was humanity's mother. Her name literally meant
"giver of life." Yet the very woman who held that name
lost the ability to give life. Eve ultimately birthed
children, but accomplished only part of her purpose.
God wanted Eve to give spiritual life.

What ever happened to Eve?

Although Eve was full of glory, deception enveloped
her. She was tempted by cunning speech and seduced
away from her original purpose. The serpent
convinced Eve to replace the King of Glory with
herself.

The devil told Eve, "You will not surely die," but his
language could not have been more deceiving. The
plurality of Hebrew language suggests Eve would
die a "double death," literally *"die-die."* Eve not only
inherited a physical death, but also lost fellowship with
the living God.

What ever happened to Eve?

Ironically the Serpent is attempting the same thing
today. He is persuading us to defy our maker; placing

ourselves in the center. Satan wants us to put our own attitudes and opinions above the will of God.

Do you give life or do you take it? What flows out of you, springs of living water or sewer runoff? Do you encourage or criticize? Are you fixated on your needs or do you consider the burdens of others? Ultimately we must be ready to acknowledge the reality of spiritual barrenness.

Eve was Banished

"So the LORD God banished them from the Garden of Eden to work the ground." Genesis 3: 23

The Garden of Eden was surely one of the most beautiful places men ever resided. Its abundance and provision is unequaled throughout history. Plowing was of no concern since God ripened luscious fruit and vegetables. Preparation of garments was unnecessary since every need was met in the Garden. The Garden of Eden was truly the most wonderful of homes.

As sin entered, Eve and her husband lost the safety and security of the place God prepared for them. They were evicted from the only home they ever knew. A couple losing their home underscores the struggle of humanity. We all long to return to a place of safety and provision.

What ever happened to Eve?

Shockingly, the scandal grows. Eve was banished not only from the Garden, but from the manifest presence of God. Leaving the Garden was one thing, but leaving the intimacy of God is something else entirely. Eve and her husband enjoyed wonderful fellowship with their Creator, but it only became a memory after the serpent was heeded.

One couple who intimately knew God - sinned and forfeited the sacredness of their relationship. Although salvaging the relationship, the closeness would never be like it once was. The Psalmist declares, *"Who may ascend the hill of the Lord? Who may stand in His holy place? He who has clean hands and a pure heart"* Psalm 24:3-4a.

Whatever happened to Eve?

The loss of innocence drives us from the glorious presence of God. Have you experienced "banishment?" Does silence echo through the empty chambers of your heart? Do you long to return to the arms of God?

Application Questions

- Describe the earliest relationship between the first family and God.

- What replaced honesty and openness in Eve's life?

- Explain why betrayal is so horrific.

- Describe the loss Eve and her husband experienced as a result of their choices.

- What attributes are reflected in our lives when selfishness fills our hearts?

> *Lord, I pray you would restore innocence in my life! Break the deception in my heart and mind. Show me the hypocrisy in my life and give me a heart of repentance. Your presence is what I long for! How I hunger for your glory in my life. Replace the gapping emptiness with your presence.*

Chapter Two:

Paradise Lost

"Satan has got men fast asleep in sin and that it is his great device to keep them so. He does not care what we do if he can do that. We may sing songs about the sweet by and by, preach sermons and say prayers until doomsday, and he will never concern himself about us, if we don't wake anybody up."

— Catherine Booth (1829-1890)

"BUT I AM AFRAID THAT JUST AS EVE WAS
DECEIVED BY THE SERPENT'S CUNNING, YOUR
MINDS MAY SOMEHOW BE LED ASTRAY FROM
YOUR SINCERE AND PURE DEVOTION TO
CHRIST." 2 CORINTHIANS 11:3

Since that fateful day in the Garden, all of humanity
has experienced loss. What happened to Eve has
happened to you and I. Without question, the tragedy
of the human condition is our loss of innocence. Oh
how I grieve our descent!

Selfish Ambition

For some time my husband and I had been grooming
a wonderful young lady to become a mouthpiece for
God in our congregation. For an extended season
we felt the Lord had been smiling down on her. The
powerful anointing and ministry giftings God placed
within her were apparent to everyone. We had great
hopes about what God was going to do through her.

This young woman had promise, but something happened on the way to her destiny. In the "wilderness" of training and preparation, her lips began to murmur. She felt she was not advancing quickly enough and being deprived of appropriate recognition. It is amazing how the serpent can deceive us with delusions of grandeur.

Ultimately this promising young woman dropped out of our congregation. Last I heard, she casually attends another congregation and is doing little for the Kingdom of God. This promising young woman's tragic story is remarkably similar to dozens of others.

Just a few years earlier a bold young man was being raised up to lead evangelism in our congregation. Virtually every time he spoke "electricity" could be felt throughout the room. Although possessing incredible gifting, he had difficulty waiting on God. Shortly before walking into his destiny, he abruptly left and joined the staff of a lukewarm congregation. In a foolhardy rush to minister, he sacrificed an opportunity to impact thousands.

He is not alone. On several occasions someone was poised to take over a ministry position when selfish ambition got the best of them. They wanted prominence, but ultimately lost even what little they possessed. The future can be shipwrecked on the jagged rocks of innocence lost.

First Love Forsaken

"You have forsaken your first love. Remember the height from which you have fallen! Repent and do the things you did at first." Revelation 2:4b

With a disappointing flick of the quill, the Apostle John penned, *"You have forsaken your first love."* Initially this admonition may have appeared a little unjustified to his listeners. After all, they labored and persevered for the sake of the Gospel. The Ephesians did much, but in the midst of their labor, Jesus was forgotten.

I found modern believers are not all that different from the Ephesians. Much of the twenty-first century church has lost the joy of its first love. We have established our vast array of programs for the evangelization of the world, but have lost a pure and sincere devotion for Jesus. It's sad we hold so much potential, but accomplish so little. It's a modern day tragedy that plays out every Sunday.

In the midst of pressures and responsibilities, have you lost the joy of your first love? Perhaps you should take a moment to examine your heart. Is Jesus still the center of your life? Misplaced love is the tainted fruit of innocence lost.

Bitter Root

"See to it that no one misses the grace of God and that no bitter root grows up to cause trouble and defile many." Hebrews 12:15

My own story is not unlike the other stories recounted. The Lord graced me with an almost idyllic childhood. I had a wonderful home with two of the most endearing parents a child could ever hope for. My mother and father cherished me every waking moment. Even though my childhood was wonderful, somehow I allowed bitterness and anger to germinate. Inadvertently, flaws were nurtured and decades saw them take root. Soon they strangled the innocence of my heart.

When I met my husband in college, I deceived the poor guy. While dating I pretended to be sweet and loving, but the moment the ring was on my finger the real Kathy was unveiled. He discovered a bitter, angry woman unlike he had known.

Six months into marriage my husband and I encountered the Holy Spirit. Shortly thereafter we were launched into full-time ministry. Although experiencing breakthroughs, I was unable to eradicate the inner turmoil. Bitterness, pride and arrogance continued to permeate the chambers of my heart.

I held on to unrealistic expectations about my husband. I expected him to bring happiness and fill every void in my life. Rather than rejoicing in a partner I could share my life with, I wanted a superhero. After several years, my husband gave up on attaining a healthy relationship and resigned himself to tolerating my foolishness. My root of bitterness was bringing alienation and the destruction of relationships.

In the grip of bitterness, I also struggled with my relationship with my daughter. Although buying designer clothes and giving her virtually every material thing, I was never really there for her. I didn't mother her from my heart. An uncomfortable silence extended into years. I discovered that the cultivation of bitterness smothers the most precious of relationships.

Bitterness also ensnared relationships with people in our congregation. I had to hide behind a massive wall of religion so I would not be seen as I really was. My greatest fear was that a member of our congregation would see the reality of my heart. While leading praise and worship, bitterness and anger pulsated. I found it difficult to be in tune with the Lord. When I told the congregation, "Let's lift holy hands to the Lord," a voice inside me said, "You hypocrite!" The condition of my life was horrible.

Although I had the Word of God in my head, it was not getting in my heart. I would repent and shove the "monster" down, but soon it would be unleashed once more. Constantly trying to be good, I lived a life of self-effort. I would cry out to God saying, "Change me! I don't want to live like this!" Yet, whenever I asked God for help, a lying voice would try to discourage me. It would proclaim, "You had better learn to accept yourself because this is who you are." Satan always tries to keep us from changing.

When would I ever be free from this grip? Would I ever see the restoration of innocence in my life? Would I be able to re-establish a good relationship with my husband and daughter? Could I ever become truly transparent with other Christians? These questions resonated in my heart.

Application Questions

- How does selfish ambition bring compromise?

- How is the Church affected by selfish ambition?

- What would happen to your life if you were to "repent and do the things you did at first?"

- Do you have a root of bitterness in your life?

> *Holy Spirit, guard my heart from selfish ambitions. I choose to humble myself, rather than seeking a position. I need to know if there is any bitterness in my heart. Lord, free me so I can love you as I did in the beginning.*

Chapter Three:

The Dowry

"Behold what God hath wrought! It is marvelous in our eyes."

— *Agnes N. Ozman (1870-1937)*

"MAKE THE PRICE FOR THE BRIDE AND THE GIFT
I AM TO BRING AS GREAT AS YOU LIKE, AND I'LL
PAY WHATEVER YOU ASK ME. ONLY GIVE ME THE
GIRL AS MY WIFE." GENESIS 34:12

Vivid storybooks grip our imagination. How we long
for distant lands where dreams come true. I recently
watched young girls at a birthday party dance and
sway in long lacy dresses. Surely they dreamed of
becoming Cinderella and being carried off by Prince
Charming.

This type of romantic daydreaming is quite prevalent
in our culture and is certainly not exclusive to
children. I have found that many of us dream of
seeing our lives transformed, moving from "peasants"
to "royalty." It is the cry of the soul to be free. Like
Cinderella, we long to be rescued and transported to
the palace of the King.

The irony of this youthful imagining is that it has a
basis of reality. Jesus, our great Prince, has come, paid
the price and rescued us from the clutches of darkness.

He has carefully prepared for us radiant garments of salvation, fine jewels and given us the oil of the Spirit for beautification.

Price for A Worthy Bride

"Give me my wife…whom I betrothed to myself for the price of…" 2 Samuel 3:14b

Throughout the Mediterranean world, men desiring a wife would be required to pay a special price to the maiden's father. This financial arrangement has often been referred to as a "dowry." While a beautiful or talented young woman could fetch a rather large dowry, an unattractive woman could barely garnish a meager one. The more beautiful and comely the woman was, the more expensive the dowry.

If a suitor was pleased with her ravishing beauty, he would willingly pay almost any amount for her hand in marriage. A bride's value to her husband was considered in the terms of her dowry. Ever a powerful picture, the dowry speaks of provision, virtue and covenant.

Scripture weaves a beautiful tapestry of the bridegroom eagerly paying a price for the bride. Isaac, the great Patriarch, joyfully paid a sizable dowry for the hand of Rebekah. Recounting this exchange, the Old

Testament declares, "… *the servant brought out gold and silver jewelry and articles of clothing and gave them to Rebekah; he also gave costly gifts to her brother and to her mother*" Genesis 24:53.

Rebekah had shown remarkable kindness and consideration. She displayed a loyalty and faithfulness to a bridegroom she had not yet gazed upon, *"Isaac brought her into the tent of his mother Sarah, and he married Rebekah. So she became his wife, and he loved her"* Genesis 24:67. Rebekah was a worthy bride and Isaac loved her.

Price For an Unworthy Bride

"The LORD said to me, 'Go show your love to your wife again, though she is loved by another and is an adulteress. Love her as the Lord loves the Israelites, though they turn to other gods and love the sacred raisin cakes.' So I bought her for fifteen shekels of silver and about a homer and a lethek of barley. Then I told her, 'You are to live with me many days; you must not be a prostitute or be intimate with any man, and I will be with you.'"
Hosea 3:1-3

While Rebekah was a worthy bride, the Bible also recounts a tragic story of an unworthy bride. The Prophet Hosea's wife received the name "Gomer" and is one of the worst bridal examples found in the Scriptures. Just a few short years after Hosea married her and began to care for her children — she was unfaithful. This blessed woman ran from the gentle hand of her husband and prostituted herself among the shadows. Hosea wrote, "*I will not show my love to her children, because they are the children of adultery. Their mother has been unfaithful and has conceived them in disgrace. She said, 'I will go after my lovers, who give me my food and my water, my wool and my linen, my oil and my drink.'" Hosea 2:4-5*. Gomer sought the pleasures of sin rather than remaining faithful to her husband.

Gomer's indiscretion mirrored Israel's infidelity. They had turned from their "husband" and became entangled with the gods of other nations. Israel's infidelity naturally grieved the heart of God. Like a betrayed husband he declared, "*Rebuke her, for she is not my wife, and I am not her husband. Let her remove the adulterous look from her face and the unfaithfulness…" Hosea 2:2b*

The ultimate outcome of this story is rather shocking. Hosea purchases back his unfaithful spouse who is now the property of another man. He releases her from the clutches of captivity and brings her back into the safety of their home. Hosea wrote, "*I bought her for fifteen shekels of silver and about a homer and a lethek of barley. Then I told her, "You are to live with me many days; you must not be a prostitute or be intimate with any man, and I will live with you." Hosea 3:2b-3.* Just when things appeared their darkest, Hosea purchased back his unfaithful bride.

Gomer was enslaved and had no hope in redeeming herself. She had to learn how to lean on the grace and mercy of her husband. In doing so, Gomer experienced salvation.

Embracing Jesus, the Last Adam

"The first man Adam became a living being; the last Adam, a life-giving spirit. The spiritual did not come first, but the natural, and after that the spiritual. The first man was of the dust of the earth, the second man from heaven. As was the earthly man, so are those who are of the earth; and as is the man from heaven, so also are those who are of heaven. And just as we have borne the likeness of the earthly man, so shall we bear the likeness of the man from heaven." 1 Corinthians 15:45b-49

Many husbands are not willing to pay the price for the welfare of their wives. Have you ever been around a husband who cares only for himself; never considering the needs of his family? I recently heard a man verbally abuse his wife in a grocery store. Another man I knew would rather spend time on the golf course than spend time with his family. Our world is littered with men who have failed as husbands.

As a husband, the first Adam failed. Although equipped to take dominion, the first Adam shrank back. Our valiant hero failed to protect his wife from works of darkness. Instead of speaking the word of God, he remained silent. While provision and hope was in his grasp, he only brought a dismal future.

Where the first Adam failed, the last Adam succeeded. The Lord and Savior Jesus Christ is our Last Adam. Not only has He paid the price of our "dowry," but he has also purchased us back from enslavement. Through the price of His shed blood we are free. As the Apostle Paul so eloquently affirmed, *"You are not your own; you were bought at a price" 1 Corinthians 6:19b-20a.*

Hearts need not be saddened, for our wondrous Bridegroom has come. Jesus Christ is our great hope and deliverer. The price He paid for the hand of His bride is immeasurable. Restored beauty awaits her.

Application Questions

- How does the story of Cinderella reflect the longings of the human heart?

- Describe how a "worthy bride" was obtained by the bridegroom.

- What was so incredible about Hosea's purchase?

- Are there things in your life that brings shame to the Lord? If so, what are they?

- How has Jesus proven to be a righteous bridegroom?

- Do you have a personal story of deliverance and redemption? If so, what is it?

Lord, I long to experience the innocence of a true bride. Wash me clean of my foolish choices. Forgive me for allowing the cares of the world to crowd you out. I am so grateful that you have redeemed my life. I give my life to you and commit myself to serve you only.

Chapter Four:

Innocence Restored

"It is time to wake up from the sleep of death and call on God to give you life."

— *Maria Woodworth-Etter (1884-1924)*

"COMFORT ALL WHO MOURN, AND PROVIDE
FOR THOSE WHO GRIEVE IN ZION— BESTOW ON
THEM A CROWN OF BEAUTY INSTEAD OF ASHES,
THE OIL OF GLADNESS INSTEAD OF MOURNING,
AND A GARMENT OF PRAISE INSTEAD OF A SPIRIT
OF DESPAIR." ISAIAH 61:2B – 3A

Confronting the "Personalities"

A frightening woman was standing before me in the front of our sanctuary. Without question, she was troubled. It wasn't just sadness or depression hanging on her, but mental instability. Although obviously driven by forces outside of her, I could see a cry for help rising up from the depths of her eyes.

This troubled young woman told me she had fourteen different personalities and had been seeing a psychologist. It was clear she wanted to have a normal life again free from demonic influence. Several prayer warriors and I gathered around to pray. In the midst of intense prayer, she began to change personalities. We got down to the very last one and it said, "I don't have to leave, I am the big one." I said, "God is bigger! Go, in the name of Jesus!" Suddenly, a tormented woman regained her innocence. She remains free to this day.

While not everyone struggles with the same things the young woman battled, they still struggle with loss of innocence. Jesus, our glorious redeemer, wants to reach out and restore innocence. By the power of His Spirit, He wants to bring us back into that special place of His presence.

Confronting the "Taskmaster"

"Captives also enjoy their ease; they no longer hear the slave driver's shout. The small and the great are there, and the slave is freed from his master."
Job 3:18

A woman in our congregation had her innocence stolen in another way. The loss ultimately affected her entire family. This woman was driven by what may be best described as a *"taskmaster spirit."* In the recesses of her mind the *"spirit"* would scream, *"It's not good enough! It's never going to be good enough! You are lazy!"*

Frustrated and driven, peace in her home was shattered as orders were barked out like a drill sergeant. As she walked into the house, harsh demands pushed everyone into a frazzled, frustrated state. Ultimately the family became disconnected.

In the midst of intensive prayer Jesus revealed the "*taskmaster spirit*." A prayer warrior declared, "*I break this thing that drives you… you relentless, unmerciful thing…let go of her now! I pull that whip out of your hand and command you to go!*" Once revealed, the "*taskmaster's*" hold was broken. She felt the power of the Holy Spirit ignite her soul. For the first time in years, she felt alive. Innocence was reawakened and a family transformed.

What have you allowed to grip your life? Are you driven by something outside of yourself? God does not want you to be overcome by evil. He wants you to live your life free from the "*slave driver's shout.*"

Confronting the "Voices"

"*In the synagogue there was a man possessed by a demon, an evil spirit. He cried out at the top of his voice, 'Ha! What do you want with us, Jesus of Nazareth? Have you come to destroy us? I know who you are—the Holy One of God!' 'Be quiet!' Jesus said sternly. 'Come out of him!'* " Luke 4:33-35a

A lovely young woman in our congregation slipped into deep depression. Over several months she heard "voices" telling her to kill herself. You could see the darkness slowly creeping into her life. Without divine intervention, I was afraid something severe might happen.

As revival burst into our congregation, we discovered the power of the Spirit brought instantaneous deliverance. So we began to violently intercede for this woman. With a fire blazing in our eyes, we would pray, *"In the name of Jesus, I command the voices to be muzzled. Be free!"*

Over the course of three or four services, a bound woman found glorious freedom. Fear and intimidation were stripped away. Her life was transformed. It was not very long before she joined our prayer ministry team. Now she helps bring the same deliverance to countless others.

Has the darkness of depression clouded your vision? Do you hear "voices" telling you to take your life? Even in the midst of shadows, God wants to bring deliverance!

Alas, The Last Eve

*"She is clothed with strength and dignity; she
can laugh at the days to come. She speaks with
wisdom, and faithful instruction is on her tongue.
Proverbs 31:25*

A transformation is taking place. A woman once prone
to deception has now taken on a mantle of wisdom
and strength. The failures of yesterday have drifted
away like dust in the wind. This woman laughs with a
seasoned heartiness and speaks with unequaled stature.
She is the "Last Eve."

In days gone by she was gripped by sin and
inadequacies, but has now found the strength to
overcome. In the conflicting shadows of life, the "Last
Eve" is guileless and uninhibited. Innocence has been
restored in her life.

The "Last Eve" is full of awe and wonder; unmarred
by the evil surrounding her. She has wisdom but is not
cynical. She is practical but not scornful. She is loving
but not fearful of being open to love.

The "last Eve" is gripped with a devotion that resounds
through time and eternity. Being passionately in love
with Jesus, she lives to bring honor to His name. Her
virtue and splendor is unsurpassed among women.

With great wisdom King Solomon wrote, "a *woman who fears the LORD is to be praised" Proverbs 31:30b.*

Return to Innocence

"Do everything without complaining or arguing. Then you will be innocent and without any wrong. You will be God's children without fault. But you are living with crooked and mean people all around you, among whom you shine like stars in the dark world." Philippians 2:14-15 NCV

Despite my best efforts, bitterness and anger continued to grip my life. In 1996, a glorious outpouring of the Holy Spirit came and I found myself in a very difficult position. Although many in our church was experiencing the Lord afresh, I had difficulty leaping into the move of God. Wrong attitudes were inhibiting my ability to fully experience the revival. After ten months my husband came with tears in his eyes saying, "Kathy, I was born for this hour. I am walking into my destiny, but you are rejecting the power of God. We are going two different directions and if this continues, you are going to miss this revival." These piercing words were spoken with tenderness and sorrow.

Suddenly the fear of God came and I received a deep realization of my deceitfulness. As self-justification shattered, I sought intense prayer. Anointed women in our congregation gathered around to pray. They cried, "Jesus, plunge your hand into Kathy's soul. Grab that bitter root and rip it out." I collapsed on the floor and could immediately feel intense "movement" in my inner being.

A wrestling match was being waged for my soul. When the dust settled, it was discovered that Jesus was the victor. The presence of God saturated me and that bitter angry root was pulled up from my heart. By God's grace, I have been free ever since.

Shortly thereafter my daughter wrote, "For so many years, I just wanted you to love me and to really mother me. But I knew you could not. Now I see you are so changed. All I want to do now is walk hand and hand with you and serve Jesus. When I have a little girl I want her to be just like you.

Application Questions

- Are there areas in your life where you are driven by something outside of yourself?

- What "voices" are given permission to speak into your mind and heart?

- What was the first step Kathy took toward freedom?

- What is the common denominator in the restoration of innocence in all of these accounts?

- Describe the transformation of the Last Eve.

Lord, I long for greater freedom! I only want to hear your voice! Separate from me from wickedness and everything that is not of you. Lord, I choose to exchange my weakness for your wisdom. I open myself to your love. Let a passion for your Kingdom possess me all the days of my life!

Chapter Five:

Realizing our Purpose

I see the new creation rise
I hear the speaking blood;
It speaks! Polluted nature dies!
Sinks 'neath the crimson flood.
I rise to walk in heav'n's own light,
Above the world and sin,
With heart made pure and garments white,
And Christ enthroned within.
Amazing grace! 'Tis heav'n below,
To feel the blood applied,
And Jesus, only Jesus know,
My Jesus crucified.

—Phoebe Palmer (1807-1874)

"AND WE KNOW THAT IN ALL THINGS GOD
WORKS FOR THE GOOD OF THOSE WHO LOVE
HIM, WHO HAVE BEEN CALLED ACCORDING TO
HIS PURPOSE." ROMANS 8:28

"Whoosh!" I watched in amazement as the power of
God swept through the room like a barreling tornado.
"Aah!" To the left and the right of me dozens were
struck down in the power of God. Groans and shrieks
pierced the auditorium as deliverance came. With
bodies strewn everywhere, the scene almost looked
like a battlefield. I have read the accounts of the Cane
Ridge Revival where similar experiences were noted.
One participant wrote,

> *"I saw at least five hundred swept down in a
> moment as if a battery of a thousand guns had
> been opened upon them, and then immediately
> followed shrieks and shouts that rent the very
> heavens."* [7]

With all the things the Lord is doing, it feels like my life is leaping off the pages of a revival history book.

Over the last several years the Holy Spirit has moved in ways I never imagined possible. Right before my eyes countless miracles have been wrought by the hand of God. Tumors have been dissolved, backs straightened and arthritis alleviated. I have witnessed hundreds of marriages on the verge of divorce rescued and thousands of troubled ministry leaders restored to effective ministry. Although overjoyed about walking into my God-ordained purpose, there are things that continue to unsettle me.

I am certain God wants people brought into His purpose, yet I have found much aimlessness and lack of vision in the Body of Christ. Christians are drifting along like a ship at sea. God wants his people to be powerful and effective, but we are wandering around in a stupor. God is eager to draw everyone into His plan. God initiates and has called us to participate.

Fan into Flame

"For this reason I remind you to fan into flame the gift of God, which is in you through the laying on of my hands. For God did not give us a spirit of timidity, but a spirit of power, of love and of self-discipline." 1 Timothy 1:6-7

I believe God has placed purpose and giftedness in the life of every Christian. While each is unique in their calling, all are called. My husband says, "I have never met a believer who is not called." God desires each of us to live up to our full potential. Yet, I found few leave the past behind and rise to the full stature God has called them to walk into.

Eric Nuzum was a forklift driver in a factory near our church. Although God gifted him with an incredible musical talent, he never lived up to his ministry potential. Living a rather uneventful life, Eric was trapped in the monotony of selfish pursuits. His beautiful voice was silenced in the darkened chambers of innocence lost.

Everything changed in the life of Eric Nuzum as the Holy Spirit ignited his heart. He responded to the outpouring power of God. Self-reliance left and innocence was restored. Eric became the worship leader of the Smithton Outpouring and now his music can be heard in over one hundred and fifty nations. Eric stepped into his destiny. Are you ready to step into yours?

Walking Into Their Destiny

*"Therefore, since we are surrounded by such a
great cloud of witnesses, let us throw off everything
that hinders and the sin that so easily entangles."
Hebrews 12:1*

People have told me, "I could never do anything for
the Kingdom of God. I've had too difficult a life and
made too many mistakes." God doesn't care how badly
you messed things up. He can bring success from the
greatest of failures. Throughout history God enabled
the most unlikely of people to walk into a glorious
destiny. Perhaps their gripping stories will challenge
you to not lose heart.

Maria Woodworth Etter

Maria Woodworth-Etter (1884-1924) had numerous
obstacles as she received the calling of the Lord in her
life. At 35 years of age, her situation seemed hopeless.
Etter possessed neither adequate Biblical knowledge
nor ministry training. She was plagued with a
deranged husband, personal illness and the death of
five of her children. It seemed she would never walk
into her destiny. Etter noted,

*"In all these trials God was preparing me and
opening the way for the great battle against the*

enemy of souls and now the great desire of my
heart was to work for Jesus…I was not qualified
for God's work. I knew that I was but a worm." [8]

Etter began to seek the Lord with a reckless abandon.
The power of God swept over her and changed her
entire life. Her problems did not go away, but they no
longer hindered her. Etter continued,

"I asked God to give me the power he gave the
Gallilean fishermen - to anoint me for service. I
came like a child asking for bread. I looked for
it… God did not disappoint me. The power of
the Holy Ghost came down like a cloud. It was
brighter than the sun. I was covered and, wrapped
in it. I was baptized with the Holy Ghost, and
Fire, and power, which has never left me. There
was liquid fire, and the angels were all around me
in fire and glory." [9]

Maria Woodworth-Etter's ministry ignited as she
approached forty years of age. Traveling the country
in an eight-thousand-seat tent, her meetings were
punctuated with remarkable signs and wonders.
Despite the most deplorable of conditions, Maria
Woodworth-Etter was able to walk into her destiny.

Aimee Semple-McPherson

Aimee Semple-McPherson (1890 - 1944) has a very similar story. Several tragedies and foolish mistakes threatened to thwart her destiny. While on the mission field in China her first husband, Robert McPherson, died. Aimee was pregnant, penniless and alone in a foreign country. Her situation appeared hopeless. She wrote,

> *"Have you ever had a secret tucked away in the closet of your Christian experience which you shrank from exposing to the sunlight of public gaze and criticism?... The year which followed my return home found me battling against the swift contrariwise tide; struggling to keep my feet, and to take up the broken thread of my life where it last left off."* [10]

The Spirit of God came to a woman in distress and brought great strength and provision. In the most unlikely of positions, Aimee found a wondrous innocence restored. She declared,

> *"Instantly light streamed over my soul. I had a peculiar sensation of something warm, cleansing and healing flowing over me from head to foot, and the great peace, the 'peace that passeth understanding', flooded my heart. My fear was*

gone and in its place was a blessed rest and sense of security." [11]

Aimee Semple-McPherson went on to become the most prominent woman evangelist in the United States. In addition to founding Angelus Temple and the International Church of the Four Square Gospel, she preached to multiplied thousands across the United States. Despite challenges Aimee Semple-McPherson was able to walk into her destiny.

Kathryn Kuhlman

Kathryn Kuhlman (1907 – 1976) also experienced tragedies and disappointments. Although establishing herself as a successful preacher, Kuhlman's marriage to Evangelist Burroughs A. Waltrip almost destroyed her ministry. Prior to marrying Kuhlman, Waltrip abandoned his wife and children in Texas. Eventually word spread of Waltrip's indiscretion and Kuhlman found herself trapped in a scandal. As result she lost her pastorate and opportunity to minister anywhere else. After being married six years to Waltrip, Kuhlman could no longer handle the situation. She left him in 1944 and four years later they divorced.

Although feeling despised and rejected, Kuhlman sought the Lord and found solace in his presence. She noted,

"Kathryn Kuhlman is just a woman. No one knows better than myself, I am nothing…I am just a child of my heavenly Father because of Jesus Christ, and without the Holy Spirit I am nothing – nothing."[12]

As time was spent with the Holy Spirit, Kuhlman's ministry was transformed. For several decades Kuhlman held healing services at the First Presbyterian Church in Pittsburgh, Pennsylvania. In addition, healing services were held at the seven thousand-seat Los Angeles Shrine Auditorium. Kuhlman also produced over five hundred telecasts for the CBS Network and in 1972 Kuhlman received the first honorary doctorate from Oral Roberts University. Despite adversity, she walked into her destiny.

The grandest failures and most formidable obstacles should not be allowed to impede our destiny. God has called us to move beyond ourselves and become empowered by Him.

Walking into My Destiny

"In all these things we are more than conquerors through him who loved us." Romans 8:37

Praise and worship is escalating and the presence of God is being ushered in. Suddenly the Lord reveals

His desire for healing. While the music softens, I boldly proclaim to the congregation, "The Lord wants to heal right now! Don't miss your 'now' moment!" Immediately all over the sanctuary people race forward to receive prayer. I walk among them proclaiming, "Life! Lord, give them life!" Suddenly through an imperfect vessel God does the impossible. God brings deliverance, the restoration of marriages and the healing of bodies.

Although in full-time ministry for twenty-one years, I had been basically ineffective in helping people receive from the Lord. After the Lord removed the bitter root and restored a child-like innocence, I finally had a real ministry. It has truly been wonderful. Over the last five years numerous people shared with me, "You prayed for me and I was set free!" Others came back years later and told me, "I was delivered of oppression and I am still free!" Praise the Lord!

I rejoice in the way God has used me, but I have learned long term spiritual giftedness only comes through character. Maintaining a Christ-like innocence in our lives is a constant battle. I can assure you that without the power of the Holy Spirit, we will never become what God has called us to be. Just like others in history, I depend on the power of the Holy Spirit to carry me.

By the grace of God, I have been able to walk into my destiny. I believe the Lord wants you to walk into yours as well. He truly wants to restore innocence in your life. He wants to restore the "nakedness" the First Eve walked in. He wants your barren womb to bring forth fruit: the fruit of repentance, the fruit of righteousness and the fruit of a changed life. He wants you to regain a loyalty and devotion. He wants you to reside in the warmth and safety of his presence. He wants you for His bride.

Application Questions

- What changes occur as people are overwhelmed by the power of God?

- Does every Christian have the calling of the Lord?

- How does Eric Nuzum's story illustrate the power of innocence restored?

- What common threads run through the stories of these great women in history?

- What fruit emerged when God overshadowed the life of the author?

> *Lord, let me walk into the destiny which you have called me! I surrender to your power. I release the controls of my life and allow you to overshadow me. I embrace all that You are. Holy Spirit, may your purpose and destiny be fully realized in my life.*

Chapter Six:

Unveiled

"The Lord shall bless you and sanctify your body for His service that His name may be sanctified through you and magnified to His glory."

— Maeyken Van Deventer (1540-1573)

"WE SPEAK AS PERSONS OF SINCERITY, AS
PERSONS SENT FROM GOD AND STANDING IN HIS
PRESENCE." 2 CORINTHIANS 2:17B NRSV

A few years ago, a woman in our congregation
graciously purchased an expensive pantsuit for me as
a gift. Not long afterward a church Christmas party
was scheduled, and I decided to wear it. I spent a lot
of time getting ready for that evening, but accidentally
put the pants on backwards. The entire evening I
walked around the party with my pants reversed.
Finally the woman who purchased the outfit whispered
in my ear, "Kathy, you are the only person in the
world who can wear a pair of pants backwards." I
immediately looked down and noticed my error.

Self-conscious and embarrassed, I walked over to
the corner of the room and covered myself with a
coat. With heat turned up in the room, sweat started
pouring down my face. Several noticed and offered
to take my coat, but I didn't want anyone to see the
mistake I had made. For the rest of the night I tried to
hide, not wanting anyone to notice what I had done.

Disguising Our Lives

"So Saul disguised himself, putting on other clothes…" 1 Samuel 28:8a

I found my experience is not unique. Everyone tries to hide failings. We endlessly labor to make ourselves look good. In a vain attempt to save face, things are hidden from friends, our boss and our spouse. While we cover the bad things, slowly everything in our life becomes hidden. Over time we develop a habit of disguise.

Relationships are built on vulnerability and disclosure. As people hide their lives, the ability to relate is hindered. It is like we are interacting with actors rather than real people. Behind "rubber masks," friendships falter and marriages dissolve. Somehow loneliness is felt in the midst of the crowd.

If we are not careful, our personal relationships become artificial and wither. The same thing hinders ministry. Many Christians are unable to impact the world because of hypocrisy. While the Church is saying all the right things, unbelievers are unable to see beyond the unauthentic lives.

Our problem is not just sin, but an inability to expose our lives. Somewhere along the way, we have become "fake." It is not enough to just experience a spiritual breakthrough, we must be transparent. We need transparency if we are going to touch people God has brought into our path.

Sewing Fig Leaves

"…they sewed fig leaves together and made coverings for themselves." Genesis 3:7

Sin entered in the midst of paradise. With a startling realization of evil, Eve covered herself. No longer was the mother of humanity comfortable displaying "nakedness." She began to hide behind hastily sewn leaves.

The tragic cover up has not ended. Trying to keep people from seeing the true condition of our lives, we hide behind money, education and religion. In an effort to convince people of our significance, we get a trendy hairstyle and purchase a brand new outfit. We attend another conference, take another course. A pretty good show is going on, but God can see behind it. The writer of Hebrews noted,

"Nothing in all creation is hidden from God's sight. Everything is uncovered and laid bare

before the eyes of him to whom we must give account." Hebrews 4:13

Thus the problem is not just our sin, but our artificiality. Turn on your television and watch the "plastic" people with perfectly-combed toupees, souped-up shoulder pads and sparkling dentures. In their blaring artificiality, we are told how to live life to the fullest. I think there is nothing more disturbing. The Apostle Paul wrote,

He will bring to light what is hidden in darkness and will expose the motives of men's hearts. 1 Corinthians 4:5b

I don't know who we think we are fooling. Maybe we only fool ourselves. A day will come when the truth of our lives will be laid bare for all to see. No longer will we be able to hide. God is going to bring to light all that which resides in darkness.

There is a young man in our church whose father had been a pastor in another congregation. Growing up, his father gave the appearance of being a godly man. Throughout the town people spoke of his kindness and charity. He was invited to speak in other congregations and held a place of prominence in the community. To most observers he appeared to be an anointed minister. Few were aware he lived a double life.

Beyond the inquiring eyes of the community, immorality seethed. He became involved in several extramarital affairs. Over time, the sin began to tear at the fabric of his very being. When his sins were finally exposed, people were astounded. This revelation particularly shattered his son, who was confronted with a man he did not know. When God brings an unveiling, what will people discover about your life?

God made us for "Nakedness"

"The man and his wife were both naked, and they felt no shame." Genesis 2:25

In the beginning the man and woman stood naked before God. Their nakedness paralleled the very innocence of their hearts. No façade or pretense dictated their relationships or conversation. Their lives were lived in truth and sincerity. This was the way God intended for it to be.

Innocence is much more than shamelessness; it is also allowing ourselves to be seen for who we really are. Being transparent keeps us vulnerable and innocent. We are to be as guileless as a child, so others can see right through us.

God wants us to live exposed, vulnerable lives. He wants us continually striving toward authenticity and being ever transformed into the likeness of Christ. The Apostle Paul alludes to this when he wrote the following,

> *"And we, who with unveiled faces all reflect the Lord's glory, are being transformed into his likeness with ever-increasing glory, which comes from the Lord, who is the Spirit." 2 Corinthians 3:18*

Where are our unveiled faces?

The Unveiling of Innocence

"Therefore be…innocent as doves." Matthew 10: 16

A reckless woman came to the revival services at our church. The very moment she entered the building, attention was drawn to her. She was immodestly dressed with a tight blouse and miniskirt that left little to the imagination.

There was an obvious heaviness resting on this woman. Although growing up in church, she had somehow got caught up in sin. Drugs, depression and demonic activity were controlling her life. We gathered around her and prayed. Soon the power of the Holy Spirit came and pierced her heart.

A little later in the service, an opportunity was given for her to testify. With miniskirt and all, she declared to our congregation, "The Lord has broken through in my life, but I am almost embarrassed to stand up in front of you. I am not worthy to be in the glory of God because of the life I have lived." With tear-drenched sincerity, it was obvious she wasn't trying to hide the condition of her life. In brutal honesty, she was unveiled before God and man. A tainted woman found innocence restored.

Application Questions

- Why is transparency so critical in relationships?

- How does lack of transparency in our lives impact the world around us?

- What are the "fig leaves" you hide behind?

- In what way were we created to be?

- Does your life reflect a "brutal honesty" before God and man?

Lord, transform my life! I want no pretenses, no facades. Shine your light in every corner of my life. Reveal the things I am trying to hide. I pray you will allow innocence to permeate my life.

Chapter Seven:

The Engagement

"Give me the love that leads the way,
The faith that nothing can dismay,
The hope no disappointments tire,
The passion that will burn like fire,
Let me not sink to be a clod
Make me Thy fuel, Flame of God."

— Amy Wilson Carmichael (1867-1951)

"HIS BRIDE HAS MADE HERSELF READY. FINE
LINEN, BRIGHT AND CLEAN, WAS GIVEN HER TO
WEAR." REVELATION 19:7B-8A

The months had been unusually frantic. We
desperately scrambled to get everything ready for my
daughter Bobbie's wedding. Invitations, decorations
and cake had to be ordered. A photographer and
wedding dress had to be selected; a reception organized
and tuxedos fitted. I learned there is much preparation
that goes into a wedding.

My daughter shifted into high gear as the big day
approached. She scheduled trips to the tanning bed,
got a haircut and purchased skin treatments. No stone
was left unturned as she prepared herself to meet her
bridegroom.

On the night before the wedding, Bobbie decided one
more thing was needed to finalize her preparation. She
purchased acrylic fingernails. My husband insisted
he could help her put them on. It was the last father-

daughter activity before giving his "little girl" away. Halfway through, it became clear that neither my daughter nor my husband knew what they were doing. Lopsided, bumpy fingernails were not going to be acceptable. Steve and Bobbie ended up staying up half the night trying different removal solutions. My daughter finally fell asleep at 4 a.m. with her hands in a bowl of acetone. The photo shoot was scheduled for 8 a.m. But, praise God, she made it! While humorous, this story paints a wonderful picture of the bridal preparation.

Bridal Preparation

"…a bride beautifully dressed for her husband."
Revelation 21:2b

The season between the engagement and wedding is filled with intense preparation. Many arrangements must be made in anticipation of the union. Before the vows are made, every "i" must be dotted and every "t" crossed.

In the Mediterranean culture the groom spent at least a year in preparation. He had to build an additional room on the side of his father's home and make other necessary arrangements. After things were finally ready, he swept in unannounced to carry his bride away.

The awaiting bride made her own preparations. Because of not knowing when the bridegroom would arrive, she had to be constantly ready. Perfumes were rubbed in and oils applied. Jewels and wedding garments were carefully placed. Everything had to be ready for a swift departure. Each waking moment was spent in preparation of the bridegroom's appearing.

The present day sign of the future Bride of Christ is preparation. As the wedding day approaches, it is time to cleanse ourselves and prepare our wedding garments.

Receiving an "Engagement Ring"

"Now it is God who has made us for this very purpose and has given us the Spirit as a deposit, guaranteeing what is to come."
2 Corinthians 5:5

I remember when my husband Steve presented a sparkling engagement ring over the Christmas holiday. I was absolutely thrilled. For me it reflected a tangible commitment to our relationship. The engagement ring was essentially a "down payment" on our future. It represented a promise that would be fulfilled on our wedding day.

 In the New Testament, we find the Holy Spirit given as an "engagement ring" to the Bride of Christ. Paul declares to the Corinthian believers, *"He anointed us, set His seal of ownership on us, and put his Spirit in our hearts as a deposit, guaranteeing what is to come"* 2

Corinthians 1:21b-22. He goes on to declare, *"Now it is God who has made us for this very purpose and has given us the Spirit as a deposit, guaranteeing what is to come" 2 Corinthians 5:5.* Finally Paul writes, *"…you were marked in Him with a seal, the promised Holy Spirit, who is a deposit guaranteeing our inheritance…" Ephesians 1:13b-14a.*

God has given His bride a "down payment" on the glorious promises to come. The Holy Spirit becomes a token of betrothal, given in anticipation of "marriage" at Christ's return. Through the Spirit, we receive the power to become what God has called us to be.

Receiving Beauty Treatments

"Before a girl's turn came to go in to King Xerxes, she had to complete twelve months of beauty treatments prescribed for the women, six months with oil of myrrh and six with perfumes and cosmetics." Esther 2:12

Although possessing great beauty, Esther still had to complete twelve months of intensive beauty treatments before she could stand before the King. In the Mediterranean culture, an extended time was set aside for beauty treatments before the marriage ceremony. During this intensive regimen the bride would regularly bathe, soak in oil and apply perfumes. This process would make the bride as beautiful as possible for her bridegroom.

The Bible often uses the imagery of bridal beautification. The most vivid example is found in Ezekiel 16:9-14. In this passage the Lord takes on the role as a bridegroom, providing clothing, oils, perfumes and jewels for his "bride", Israel.

> *"I bathed you with water and washed the blood from you and put ointments on you. I clothed you with an embroidered dress and put leather sandals on you. I dressed you in fine linen and covered you with costly garments. I adorned you with jewelry: I put bracelets on your arms and a necklace around your neck, and I put a ring on your nose, earrings on your ears and a beautiful crown on your head. So you were adorned with gold and silver; your clothes were of fine linen and costly fabric and embroidered cloth. Your food was fine flour, honey and olive oil. You became very beautiful and rose to be a queen. And your fame spread among the nations on account of your beauty, because the splendor I had given you made your beauty perfect, declares the Sovereign LORD." Ezekiel 16:9-14*

God wants to adorn us with rich garments, anoint us with oil and array us with jewelry. He has provided everything we need to walk into our destiny. Are you willing to go through the process? Let us say "*yes*" to Jesus and forever affirm our desire to become whatever He wants us to be.

Adorned With Rich Garments

"Now Joshua was dressed in filthy clothes as he stood before the angel. The angel said to those who were standing before him, 'Take off his filthy clothes.' Then he said to Joshua, 'See, I have taken away your sin, and I will put rich garments on you.'" Zechariah 3:3-4

Like a woman clothed in wedding attire, the Bride of Christ is being draped in the garments of righteousness. Casting away soiled fabrics of innocence lost, she puts on a brand new dress. This beautiful clothing did not come from her hand, but as a gift from the Bridegroom.

"*Rich garments of salvation*" have been provided for the Bride of Christ. Representing so much more than a home in heaven, salvation brings safety from danger, restoration of health and material provision. Those adorned in garments of salvation can experience abundant life in the here and now.

Yet, in order to be clothed with garments of righteousness, the soiled garments of our past must be removed. For most, leaving the past requires a powerful encounter with God. Some are like Lazarus coming out of the tomb with the grave clothes still gripping their resurrected life. Paul tells us, "*... to put off your old self, which is being corrupted by its deceitful desires; to be made new in the attitude of your minds;*

and to put on the new self, created to be like God in true righteousness and holiness" Eph 4:22-24.

The filthy garments of "self-righteousness" had to be removed from my life. As long as I wore my grave clothes, I was unable to step into the purposes of God. When wrong attitudes and selfishness were stripped from my life, I was finally able to be clothed with righteousness!

As the Bride of Christ we need to put on the right clothes. In the Parable of the Wedding Banquet, the King asked a piercing question, *"How did you get in here without wedding clothes?"* Matthew 22:12b. The answer is simple. Those not wearing wedding garments are not allowed in the wedding.

Anointed With Oil

"I bathed you with water and washed the blood from you and put ointments on you." Ezekiel 16:9

Like a bride soaking in oil to nourish her skin, God is anointing the bride of Christ with the oil of the Holy Spirit. Callousness and hardness soften in the oil of His presence. For the bride, oil brings purity and consecration. The Lord said to Moses, *"Take the anointing oil and anoint the tabernacle and everything in it; consecrate it and all its furnishings, and it will be holy" Exodus 40:9.* God desires to anoint His bride with the oil.

A disillusioned pastor from the Midwest visited our congregation. Feeling like innocence and purity were being stripped from him, he lost the hope of his calling. While preaching that evening, I felt motivated by the Spirit to say, "*You may be a discouraged pastor and want to quit the ministry, but Jesus wants to pour fresh oil from heaven into your life!*" As those words went forth, he ran to the front and collapsed under the weightiness of the presence of God. As the oil of the Holy Spirit cascaded over his heart, holiness was renewed. He went back to his congregation restored with a new sense of destiny.

Several years ago my husband taught me that holiness has two sides. He said, "We are being set apart both 'for' and 'from'. We are set apart for 'God's use only', while also being set apart from the 'world'." It is time we learn that the lifestyle of holiness is essential for the fulfillment of our destiny. The writer of Hebrews reminds us that without holiness, "no one will see the Lord" Hebrews 12:14b.

Thus we have a problem. Commitment and consecration has been largely absent from American congregations. Rigid legalism and powerless form have replaced it. We have somehow allowed holiness to be reduced to a set of "do's and don'ts." Christians must gain a renewed understanding of holiness.

Have you been anointed by the oil of the Holy Spirit? Holiness was meant to be more than Biblical truth, it is meant to be an experience.

Arrayed With Jewelry

"I delight greatly in the LORD; my soul rejoices in my God. For he has clothed me with garments of salvation and arrayed me in a robe of righteousness, as a bridegroom adorns his head like a priest, and as a bride adorns herself with her jewels." Isaiah 61:10

In the Mediterranean culture, the bridegroom would often purchase jewelry for his bride. Golden earrings and a sparkling necklace would accentuate her loveliness. As she entered on their wedding day, everyone would be drawn to her beauty. Her magnificence was reflected in the splendor of her jewelry.

On a rare occasion Steve and I were able to shop at a jewelry store. In the midst of casual browsing, we spotted a very beautiful diamond ring. While examining the ring, we discovered we were not the only ones fond of the ring. The sales person was also taken with it. Since we had not planned on purchasing anything, we decided to wait.

Later, Steve gave our daughter the serial number and
sent her to purchase the ring. With great fanfare Steve
handed me the box and I opened it. Glancing down
at the stone, my countenance fell. Anticipating a
beautiful diamond, I was shocked to find one with so
many flaws. To everyone's surprise, the ring had been
switched. (The sales person was the prime suspect!) I
expected a gorgeous jewel, but the one that replaced
did not have the luster. After some phone calls, the
manager of the jewelry store gladly refunded our
money.

Fortunately, I am glad that nothing like this has
happened to the Bride of Christ. God will not
settle for imperfections in the gifts He gives us.
The wonderful gifts of the Holy Spirit beautify and
empower the Bride. Through the diversity of these
gifts, we are enabled and equipped. Whether it is
wisdom, faith, healing or power, God has given us the
provision to become everything we need to be. The
Apostle Paul affirms,

> *"There are different kinds of gifts, but the
> same Spirit... To one there is given through the
> Spirit the message of wisdom, to another the
> message of knowledge by means of the same
> Spirit, to another faith by the same Spirit, to
> another gifts of healing by that one Spirit, to
> another miraculous powers, to another prophecy,
> to another distinguishing between spirits, to
> another speaking in different kinds of tongues,*

and to still another the interpretation of tongues.
All these are the work of one and the same
Spirit, and he gives them to each one, just as he
determines." 1 Corinthians 12:4, 7-11

Are the gifts of the Spirit operating in your life? Are
you allowing the Bridegroom to array you with His
precious "jewels?"

Receiving the Friend of the Bridegroom

"The bride belongs to the bridegroom. The
friend who attends the bridegroom waits and
listens for him, and is full of joy when he hears
the bridegroom's voice. That joy is mine, and it
is now complete." John 3:29

Like a groom who sends a friend to help his bride,
God sends people to assist the Bride of Christ to
fulfill her vow. In the midst of preparations in the
Mediterranean culture, a bridegroom would often
send a devoted friend to keep an eye on his bride. The
friend of the bridegroom would assist the bride in
fulfilling her pledge. Reflecting on the purpose of the
friend of the bridegroom, Dr. David Williams noted,

"The friend of the bridegroom...acted as a
liaison between the bride and groom...The
friend of the bridegroom had a particular duty

*to…ensure that the Bride came to her wedding
as a virgin."* [13]

Reflecting on his relationship with the "Bride of
Christ", the Apostle Paul occasionally speaks as the
"Bridegroom's Friend". Paul felt a divine obligation
to help maintain the purity of the Church. In specific
reference to this role, Paul wrote,

> *"I'm jealous for you with a Godly jealousy. I promised
> you to one husband — to Christ so that I might present
> you as a pure virgin to Him."* 2 Corinthians 11:2

Just as the Apostle Paul was sent to help the Church,
God sends others to help us prepare for the coming of
the Bridegroom. Have you considered all the people
God has brought into your life? Pastors, teachers and
mentors have all been given to help you. Through
teaching, preaching and friendships, you are being
challenged to remain faithful to Jesus.

"Friends of the bridegroom" prod us on. Loyalty and
commitment are ever on their lips. Their only passion
is to see the fulfillment of the bridal vow. A friend
of the bridegroom would never say, *"Don't worry
about the wedding, go out and have fun. Enjoy yourself,
the groom will never know."* These men and women
relentlessly encourage us to remain true to Jesus.

How do you respond to *"friends of the bridegroom"*
sent to watch over your life? Do you rejoice in their
involvement or would you rather they left you alone?
We must be careful we don't become like the Laodician

Church declaring, "*I am rich; I have acquired wealth and do not need a thing*" *Revelation 3:17a.*

Loyalty in the Bridal Chamber

"Come, I will show you the bride, the wife of the Lamb." Revelation 21:9

The wedding is on, but only those who remain loyal will make it to the bridal chamber. The first Eve failed when her loyalty was tested. The deception of evil was chosen over the goodness of God. The tragedy of the Garden of Eden plays out every day as thousands walk away from their commitments.

Husbands break vows made to their families, bills aren't paid and churches split. Perhaps most unsettling is the thousands of people who pledge their lives to Jesus, only to later walk away. I don't know how someone can know His presence, call Him Lord and serve Him for a season, and then turn away.

God is coming for His Bride. The good news is you don't have to be the most attractive or the most talented. In fact, you don't even have to be the most spiritual. You only need to be the most devoted. God is looking for someone loyal to spend eternity with.

Application Questions

- In the Mediterranean culture, what preparations were made for a wedding?

- How is the Holy Spirit like an engagement ring?

- What is your responsibility in regard to "beauty treatments?"

- What does "soaking in oil" represent?

- How do gifts of the Spirit operate in the life of the believer?

- Are there any "Friends of the Bridegroom" in your life? If so, how do you respond?

- What is the single greatest quality that needs to be reflected by the Bride?

> *Lord, I want to thank you for your gracious gifts to me. Your righteousness saves me, your holiness cleanses me and your Spirit empowers me. Lord, equip me to receive each of these fully. I am desperate to have more of you! I will not rest till I look like you. You and You alone captivate my heart! I love you! Never shall I rest in my pursue of You!*

Chapter Eight:

From Barrenness to Fruitfulness

*"O Hope! Dazzling, radiant Hope! -- What a change
thou bringest to the hopeless; brightening the darkened
paths, and cheering the lonely way."*

— Aimee Semple Mcpherson (1890-1944)

"SING, O BARREN WOMAN, YOU WHO NEVER
BORE A CHILD; BURST INTO SONG, SHOUT FOR
JOY, YOU WHO WERE NEVER IN LABOR; BECAUSE
MORE ARE THE CHILDREN OF THE DESOLATE
WOMAN THAN OF HER WHO HAS A HUSBAND,"
SAYS THE LORD. "ENLARGE THE PLACE OF YOUR
TENT, STRETCH YOUR TENT CURTAINS WIDE,
DO NOT HOLD BACK; LENGTHEN YOUR CORDS,
STRENGTHEN YOUR STAKES. FOR YOU WILL
SPREAD OUT TO THE RIGHT AND TO THE LEFT;
YOUR DESCENDANTS WILL DISPOSSESS NATIONS
AND SETTLE IN THEIR DESOLATE CITIES." ISAIAH
54:1-3

My daughter Bobbie is an absolute natural with
children. She is, as one member of our congregation
recently noted, a *"kid-magnet."* Almost anytime she
is around, kids will gather. Bobbie will have a baby
sitting in her lap and another child pulling on her pant
leg. All the kids at church know her by name and love
to be around her.

Consequently, it was heartbreaking when my daughter and her husband had trouble conceiving. They tried surgery and fertility drugs, but each proved ineffective. Disappointing months slowly turned into years. Laughter did not fill their home.

My daughter's barrenness moved my heart. I watched as she literally did everything possible to have a baby. With tear-filled eyes she asked me, "Will I ever know the joy of having a child?" I tried to comfort her but to no avail. By all appearances my daughter was barren.

Be Fruitful and Multiply

"And God blessed them, and God said unto them, Be fruitful, and multiply, and replenish the earth, and subdue it: and have dominion over the fish of the sea, and over the fowl of the air, and over every living thing that moveth upon the earth." Genesis 1:28 KJV

One of the first commands God gave humanity was "*be fruitful and multiply*". Throughout the Bible, God's heart toward fruitfulness is seen. In the beginning, God declared, *"Let the earth bring forth the living creature after his kind..." Genesis 1:24b*. Later, He promised Abram, *"I will greatly increase your numbers" Genesis 17:2b*. Without question God desires fruitfulness.

While God longs for fruitfulness in the natural, He also longs for it in the spiritual. John the Baptist declared, "Produce fruit in keeping with repentance… every tree that does not produce good fruit will be cut down and thrown into the fire" Matthew 3:8b, 10b. Jesus expected fruit: "This is to my Father's glory, that you bear much fruit, showing yourselves to be my disciples…bear fruit—fruit that will last" John 15:8, 16b. In the same manner Paul writes, "We pray this in order that you may live a life worthy of the Lord and may please him in every way: bearing fruit in every good work, growing in the knowledge of God" Colossians 1:10. Fruitfulness in the spiritual as well as the natural is what God desires.

In the latter part of the 16th Century, Richard and Ann Edwards became renown throughout England for their devotion to Christ. They lived in difficult times. Despite insurmountable challenges their lives were devoted to the work of the Church. The Edwards' possessed an unswerving commitment to the Gospel and the fruit of their devotion resounds through history.

Richard and Ann produced a son named William Edwards who journeyed to America; establishing himself as a reputable businessman. Over time William Edwards also had a son, Timothy. Timothy followed in his grandfather's footsteps, becoming a prominent minister. As years passed Timothy Edwards also produced a son, Jonathan Edwards. Jonathan became a prominent leader in the Great Awakening, establishing revival in the American colonies.

In the years that followed, a multitude of godly children sprang from bloodline of Richard and Ann Edwards. The commitment one family made to Christ produced glorious fruit. Evangelist Steve Hill wrote,

> *"It is worthwhile to note one family…who lived an upright holy life before God, passed their heritage on to their children. They produced: 295 college graduates, 13 college presidents, 65 professors, 60 physicians, 108 preachers of the gospel, 101 lawyers, 30 judges, 1 Vice President of the United States, 75 Army and Navy officers, 60 prominent authors, 16 railroad and shipping presidents. In the entire record of the Edwards family history, not one had ever been convicted of a crime."* [14]

God has called us to produce good fruit. Will the glory of God still be reflected centuries after your death? Will your family be remembered for its godliness or forgotten with those who abandoned the gospel?

The Barren Womb

"Now Sarai was barren; she had no children"
Genesis 11:30

Fruitfulness is the desire of God's heart, but sin has produced barrenness in our lives. From the very moment iniquity entered into the garden, humanity lost the ability to bear spiritual fruit. While fruitfulness was God's intention, the world has become barren.

The Bible paints numerous pictures of the pain of physical barrenness. Hannah cried out to the Lord saying, *"O LORD Almighty, if you will only look upon your servant's misery and remember me, and not forget your servant but give her a son, then I will give him to the LORD for all the days of his life"* 1 Samuel 1:10B. Speaking of barrenness in terms of unceasing yearning, King Solomon wrote, *"There are three things that are never satisfied, four that never say, 'Enough!': the grave, the barren womb, land, which is never satisfied with water, and fire, which never says, 'Enough'"* Proverbs 30: 15b-16. Both passages convey the sadness and despair that can be associated with barrenness.

Over the years, a handful of women in our congregation have come to me with their problems of infertility. You could see bitterness trying to take root in their lives. While doing their best to congratulate new mothers in our congregation, you could tell jealousy was simmering. I would try to comfort them in the midst of their sorrow. But without a powerful spiritual release, that "hook" in the heart is immovable.

The Barren Woman

"I will make you very fruitful; I will make nations of you, and kings will come from you. I will establish my covenant as an everlasting covenant between me and you and your descendants after you for the generations to come, to be your God and the God of your descendants after you." Genesis 17:6

While numerous passage in the Bible deal with barrenness, perhaps the most illustrative lessons can be drawn from the story of Abram and Sarai. God promised Sarai and Abram that their offspring would possess an "everlasting covenant" with Him. Specifically this glorious promise was a son that would come through them. As God so strongly affirmed, *"…a son coming from your own body will be your heir" Genesis 15:4b.*

Seasons passed and failure came. Ultimately Sarai and her husband attempted to fulfill the promise by their own means. At Sarai's insistence, Abram slept with the maidservant Haggar.

Now Sarai, Abram's wife, had borne him no children. But she had an Egyptian maidservant named Hagar; so she said to Abram, "The LORD has kept me from having children. Go, sleep with my maidservant; perhaps I can build a family through her." Genesis 16:1-2

As result, Ishmael was conceived. While Abram held great hope about his firstborn son, he soon learned disobedience and self-effort are not blessed by God. Things which are birthed "in the flesh," will never receive God's endorsement. God only blesses that which is born "of the Spirit." A great struggle perpetually exists between that which is birthed in the Spirit and that which is birthed in the flesh. The Apostle Paul clarified this conflict when he wrote, *"...the son born in the ordinary way persecuted the son born by the power of the Spirit" Galatians 4:29b.*

It is imperative we place our trust in Jesus. He is our portion and our source. When people finally stop taking things into their own hands, the genuine fruitfulness of the Lord will be seen.

Have you placed your complete trust in him?

The Barren Church

"You say, 'I am rich; I have acquired wealth and do not need a thing.' But you do not realize that you are wretched, pitiful, poor, blind and naked." Revelation 3:17

On the Cross of Calvary, Jesus bled and died to bring forth a fruitful Church. With victorious affirmation, Jesus declared, *"upon this rock I will build my church;*

and the gates of hell shall not prevail against it" Matthew 16:18. Among Jesus' closing words was the command, *"...go and make disciples of all nations" Matthew 28:19.* From the very beginning the intention has always been for the Church to be fruitful.

While God desires fruitfulness, lethargy and blatant hypocrisy grips the Church of Jesus Christ. Across America there are many Christians who have never:

- Led anyone to Jesus.

- Experienced the real presence and glory of God.

- Heard the Shepherd's voice.

- Been able to reproduce their spiritual heart in the natural children they have reproduced.

- Been able to disciple anyone into a spiritually productive life.

My husband says the American church is sick unto death. Rather than evangelism, Church growth comes from shifting membership. According to George Barna, divorce rates among Christians are higher than non-Christians. I have to agree with the late Leonard Ravenhill when he wrote,

> *"At this grim hour the world sleeps in the darkness and the Church sleeps in the light...*

> *The limping Church militant is derisively called*
> *the Church impotent."* [15]

An evangelist friend of ours recounted a shocking story
of a pastor in Pennsylvania. The evening before the
Sunday service, the pastor noticed a dead woodchuck
in the drive of the church. The carcass was not only
full of flies and maggots, but rank with a horrendous
odor. He went to get a shovel and remove the decaying
body. Before he could scoop it up, he heard the
Spirit of God whisper; *"This is what your church looks*
like to me!" Becoming aware of how God saw his
congregation, he began to bitterly weep.

It is time we come to the realization that the Church
has failed. While being called to fruitfulness, the
people of God have become barren. A Church that
does not reproduce itself is not the Church Jesus
called.

Encountering the God of the Impossible

> *Now Sarah was listening at the entrance to*
> *the tent, which was behind him. Abraham*
> *and Sarah were already old and well advanced*
> *in years, and Sarah was past the age of*
> *childbearing. So Sarah laughed to herself as she*
> *thought, "After I am worn out and my master is*

*old, will I now have this pleasure?" Genesis 18:
10b*

God made a remarkable promise to Sarah. Yet the
"impossibility" of the situation brought an almost
irreverent response. Sarah, being well past the age of
childbearing, found herself chuckling at the notion of
pregnancy. Can Sarah really be blamed for laughing?
Has God ever made a promise that sounded so far-
fetched you laughed?

My husband and I experienced something similar.
Years ago, while pastoring in the tiny town of
Smithton, Missouri, the Lord made a startling
promise. He told me one day *Hosanna! Integrity Music*
would record our praise and worship and take it to
the nations. When I shared that promise with my
husband, he actually laughed. *"Impossible!"* he said.
Here we were in a town of 532, with a small country
church that few people wanted to visit. Steve was on
the keyboards, I was the main vocalist and we were
backed by a ragtag group of individuals. The situation
appeared pretty barren.

Revival erupted and in the winter of 1998, *Hosanna!
Integrity Music* came to see what was happening in
our midst. A year later they recorded *"The Smithton
Outpouring — Revival in the Heartland,"* featuring
songs by my husband and our worship leader, Eric
Nuzum. Widely received, it was distributed in over

one hundred and fifty nations. What once seemed impossible was now happening in our midst.

We must be continually reminded that God moves in the miraculous. He makes a roadway in the wilderness and gives water when we thirst. He provides for us abundantly when things seem hopeless. He is truly the God of the impossible.

For Sarah, the impossible broke into the world in which she lived. At the frail age of ninety, she became pregnant and brought forth a child! The Bible recounts Sarah's story in the following passage,

> *Now the LORD was gracious to Sarah as he had said, and the LORD did for Sarah what he had promised. Sarah became pregnant and bore a son to Abraham in his old age, at the very time God had promised him. Abraham gave the name Isaac to the son Sarah bore him. When his son Isaac was eight days old, Abraham circumcised him, as God commanded him. Abraham was a hundred years old when his son Isaac was born to him. Sarah said, "God has brought me laughter, and everyone who hears about this will laugh with me." And she added, "Who would have said to Abraham that Sarah*

*would nurse children? Yet I have borne him a
son in his old age." Genesis 21:1-7*

Who would have thought a barren woman could
bring forth a child? Yet, God accomplished it! From
the depths of barrenness, sprang the glorious child of
promise.

When Grace Comes

*"Isaac prayed to the LORD on behalf of his
wife, because she was barren. The LORD
answered his prayer, and his wife Rebekah
became pregnant." Genesis 25:21*

I found barrenness is the most difficult when it hits
close to home. My daughter Bobbie and her husband
desperately wanted a child. For three years they tried
to conceive, struggling through various medical
processes. Finally, their doctor sat them down and
told them, *"I am sorry, but there is nothing more I can
do for you!"* Desperate tears enveloped my daughter's
eyes as she left the doctor's office.

After striving for three years, my daughter and her
husband put their complete trust in God. Although
things appeared hopeless, they sought the Lord's
miraculous intervention. In one of the outpouring
services at our church, my daughter responded to God.
In the presence of the Holy Spirit, hope was restored.
In the midst of barrenness, a glorious miracle ensued.

Without any form of medical help, a baby girl was conceived. At the close of the twentieth century my granddaughter, Allyson Grace King, was born. She is a picture of what God will do with the church — and with you personally — as the Last Eve is allowed to break her cycle of barrenness.

Application Questions

- Does fruitfulness flow from your life?

- What choices are you making to ensure that God will be glorified for centuries after your death?

- Is there any barrenness in your life?

- What exists between the things which are birthed in the flesh and those birthed by the Spirit?

- How is the church "wretched, pitiful, poor, blind, and naked?"

- What is the only hope of one who is in a barren condition?

- Has the "God of the impossible" broken into your life? How?

Lord, let your name be honored! Let everything I do glorify your name. I want to bear fruit that comes not from fleshly efforts but from the trust I have in you. While there are impossible situations in my life, I choose to walk by faith - not by sight. Once again I want to enter into your glorious presence. Come spring up in me.

.

Chapter Nine:

In the Shadow of the Almighty

"We must walk very close to a companion if we would have His shadow fall on us."

— *Mary Duncan (1825-1865)*

"He who dwells in the shelter of the
Most High will rest in the shadow of
the Almighty. I will say of the LORD,
'He is my refuge and my fortress, my God,
in whom I trust.' Surely he will save you
from the fowler's snare and from the
deadly pestilence. He will cover you with
his feathers, and under his wings you will
find refuge; his faithfulness will be your
shield and rampart. You will not fear the
terror of night, nor the arrow that flies
by day." Psalm 91:1-5

A couple found a dog wandering the streets where they
lived. Feeling compassion for the straggly mutt, they
decided to help. At first the dog snapped and rejected
their attempts at kindness. Ultimately the dog relented
and allowed the couple to take him to their house.

After arriving in the couple's home the dog was
bathed, given a haircut and a warm place to sleep.
Every need the dog had was being met. In the confines

of a safe place, a powerful transformation took place; a dangerous animal became a cuddly pet.

In the midst of wandering, God invites us to encounter Him. He wants His creation to return to a place of safety and security. He did not create us to wander in the scorching desert, but walk with Him in the cool of the garden. Will you return to the warmth and safety of His arms?

Ruth, at the Feet of Her Redeemer

"Praise be to the LORD, who this day has not left you without a kinsman-redeemer."
Ruth 4:14b

Although the Bible gives many accounts of finding sanctuary, Ruth's story is perhaps the most poignant. Ruth was ever faithful and resourceful, even in a time of great difficulty. Lying at the feet of her redeemer, Boaz, she ultimately received the covering and provision she needed.

Ruth was Faithful

"Where you go I will go, and where you stay I will stay." Ruth 1:16b

During a time of famine and death, widows Ruth and Naomi journey back to the land of promise. Ruth easily could choose to leave Naomi's side, but remains faithful. She said, *"Don't urge me to leave you or to turn back from you. Where you go I will go, and where you stay I will stay. Your people will be my people and your God my God. [17] Where you die I will die, and there I will be buried. May the LORD deal with me, be it ever so severely, if anything but death separates you and me"* Ruth 1:16-17. While others leave, Ruth cleaves. What a beautiful example of faithfulness.

In our own times of uncertainty, how beautiful it is when we follow Ruth's example of faithfulness. As a pastor's wife for many years now, I have watched people in times of uncertainty disappear from church. As hurt is experienced they pull away from Christian friends. The next thing you know they are back to their fruitless past. Ruth's faithfulness ultimately brought her to the place of blessing.

Several years ago, a gifted couple in our congregation decided to affirm their faithfulness and commitment. They stood up in front of the entire church and declared, *"We love you and support you. No matter what happens we will never leave you or forsake you."* Their words were very moving and touched many within our congregation. However, not long after making these statements, they left our church. When our hearts don't match our words, it is only a matter of time before our faithfulness wanes. Later, when revival struck our congregation, this talented couple was not there to experience one of the greatest moves of God in history.

Ultimately faithfulness becomes a pathway to provision. When the Lord told us to move our ministry to Kansas City, there were numerous obstacles. First of all we didn't have a building in which to meet. Then a handful of people set out to do everything possible to keep us from succeeding. In the back of our minds we heard the taunts of the enemy saying, "*You are foolish. You are never going to be able to make it. You ought to just go back!*" Yet our faithfulness never waned.

My husband and I, along with most of our congregation, pulled up our roots and moved to Kansas City. We chose faithfulness to Jesus over the security of what we had known. Commitment has proven to be a blessing. Our Church has a brand new building on sixty-two acres of land. In addition to seeing exponential growth in our congregation, we have launched a ministry training center, a television broadcast and numerous other ministries. Faithfulness will always bring you into blessing.

If your life has no commitments, how can you ever hope to be blessed? As Ruth committed to the right choices, God guided her on a path to sanctuary. He will do the same for you.

Ruth was Resourceful

*"So Boaz said to Ruth, "My daughter, listen to
me. Don't go and glean in another field and
don't go away from here. Stay here with my
servant girls. Watch the field where the men
are harvesting, and follow along after the girls.
I have told the men not to touch you. And
whenever you are thirsty, go and get a drink
from the water jars the men have filled." At this,
she bowed down with her face to the ground.
She exclaimed, "Why have I found such favor
in your eyes that you notice me—a foreigner?"
Ruth 2:8-10*

Ruth is a wonderful picture of what can happen when
your back is against the wall. In a time of great need,
she became resourceful. Although trouble was all
around, she didn't just lie down and die. Ruth set out
to do everything she could to change her situation.
Knowing Israel's kindness to the fatherless and the
widow, Ruth began to glean from the remnants of
the field. Because of her relentless tenacity, she found
herself in position to meet her kinsman-redeemer.

In many ways Ruth's story becomes a mirror for our
own lives. Do you shrink back when trouble comes?
Are you incapacitated if there is a temporary lack of
safety and provision in your life? Like Ruth, we must
learn to prevail! Casting aside fear, we must learn how
to place ourselves in the right place for blessing.

Over the years people have shared with me all the things lacking in their lives. One woman told me how her husband was hindering her life. Another revealed how an inadequate education caused the loss of opportunity. The lack of money is the one I hear most often. Recently I heard someone say, *"If I only had more money, I know I could become a success."* People forget that everyone has areas in their lives that inhibit them.

In the midst of challenges, God has given grace to overcome. Forget the things you do not have and learn to do something with what you do have. Ruth had very little to work with as she entered Israel, but she learned to make the best of what she had. Through her resourcefulness, the door was opened to meet her Kinsman-Redeemer.

We must learn to be resourceful. When Christians finally learn to prevail in small endeavors, God will open the door of provision wider. After all the Bible declares, *"He who faithful in small things will be ruler over many" Matthew 25:21.* Ultimately the question is not, *"What do you have?"* but *"What are you doing with what you have?"*

Ruth was Covered

*" 'Who are you?' Boaz asked. 'I am your servant
Ruth,' she said. 'Spread the corner of your
garment over me, since you are a kinsman-
redeemer.' " Ruth 3:9*

With deepest humility and submission, Ruth placed
herself at the feet of her kinsman-redeemer. In that
position, a childless widow found a transformed
life. With a picture of provision and security, Boaz
ultimately *"spread the corner of his garment"* over Ruth.
One who was homeless would now possess a home.
One who was childless would soon possess a child.
One   was penniless would now have provision.

It is important that we learn from Ruth's example. In
order to walk into safety and security, we must learn
submission. Submission becomes a doorway into the
sanctuary of our God. The writer of Hebrews affirms,

*"Obey your leaders and submit to their
authority. They keep watch over you as men who
must give an account. Obey them so that their
work will be a joy, not a burden, for that would
be of no advantage to you." Hebrews 13:17*

When we are "under cover," we find protection and
provision. Pastors and other ministry leaders are
gifts for our good. They are God's representatives
to guide and protect the Church. When we yield to
their leadership, we can find our way to the place of
blessing.

Over the years people have come to my husband and
I, asking for a blessing on their life plans. We always
try our best to give our consent, but it is difficult
when we are not involved in the decision making
process. We want to seek the Lord with them for their
future, but if the decision has been already made, it
is difficult to give a stamp of approval. Today it is
common for people to "go" without being "sent." In
the book of Acts people never just go; they are always
sent by the local church. When people go without
being sent, it almost always ends in failure. Through
local congregations and leadership God has provided a
wonderful supernatural covering. Submission is where
we need to find ourselves.

Needless to say, countless people around the world live
"uncovered" lives. Floating from here and there, they
are unwilling to be accountable to leadership. When
trouble comes, there is no there to help them. Only
those who are under cover are able to rest in the safety
of His arms. The Psalmist affirms this reality when he
penned the following,

> *"He who dwells in the shelter of the Most High
> will rest in the shadow of the Almighty. I will
> say of the LORD, 'He is my refuge and my
> fortress, my God, in whom I trust.' Surely he
> will save you from the fowler's snare and from
> the deadly pestilence. He will cover you with
> his feathers, and under his wings you will find*

*refuge; his faithfulness will be your shield and
rampart." Psalm 91:1-2*

Are you "covered"? Are you protected by the hand of
God?

In The Presence of God

*"13 In the presence of God, who gives life to all
things" 1 Timothy 6:13 NRSV*

The nineteenth century holiness author, Hannah
Whitall Smith, penned, *"His presence is literally and
truly all we need for everything. It would be enough
for us, even if we had not a single promise nor a single
revelation of His plans."* [16] Like Hannah, we must come
to the realization that the ultimate place of safety and
provision is in the glorious presence of God.

In the Garden of Eden the manifest presence of God
was continually experienced. Eve and her husband
were enveloped by the weightiness of His glory. Yet
everything changed as Eve bit into the forbidden fruit.
Sin entered and the glory of the Lord departed. No
longer were they saturated with His presence. The
estrangement of sin replaced the intimate communion
they once had.

For years I thought I experienced the presence of God,
but I had to change my thinking when the glory of
God swept into our congregation. On March 24, 1996
a great outpouring of the Holy Spirit began in our

midst. God's presence was so real and transforming. We were astounded that we could actually feel the touch of his hand. As the Glory of the Lord settled over us like a soft blanket, our knees buckled and our burdens left. Waves of the Holy Spirit came and many collapsed under the weight of His glory. The conscious awareness of His nearness was branded on our hearts.

Since then, we never take the presence of God for granted. Week in and week out we cry out to God to keep the atmosphere of His glory here at World Revival Church. We cannot live without the presence of God. Staying in His presence maintains our innocence. When we continually allow areas of our lives to be unveiled in His presence, we are empowered and released from our sins.

I have to agree with the late Ruth Ward Heflin when she wrote, *"I want to declare, as did Moses: if God's presence goes not with me, I just don't want to go. I don't want to go where He has not gone before me in the fullness of His glory, in that manifestation of His presence."* [17]

Application Questions

- How does the account of Ruth illustrate the relationship between faithfulness and God's provision?

- Are you faithful in your life?

- What are the three ways Ruth responded when she faced adversity?

- Why is the question "What are you doing with what you have?" more critical than "What do you have?"

- What is necessary in order to walk into safety and security?

- Explain the concept of "being under cover."

- Where is the ultimate place of safety and provision?

- How have you tangibly experienced the presence of God?

   Lord, give me courage to journey into the unknown, with faithfulness and devotion. Strengthen me to become resourceful with what I have. Once again, I submit to those who have been placed in authority. My safety and security are in you Lord and I choose to remain there.

Chapter Ten:

Return to Eden

"Oh, the unspeakable happiness of belonging to Jesus Christ! Belonging to Jesus Christ is the true balm which sweetens all those pains and sorrows which are so inseparable from this earthly life."

— Jeanne Guyon (1648-1717)

"SAY TO THE DAUGHTER OF ZION, 'SURELY
YOUR SALVATION IS COMING; BEHOLD, HIS
REWARD IS WITH HIM, AND HIS WORK BEFORE
HIM.'" ISAIAH 62:11

It was surely one of the most wonderful of days. The joyous morning my daughter got married, I couldn't hold back my delight. She was beautifully adorned in a flowing white gown and translucent veil. Flowers lined the very ground she walked. Every eye in the place was fixed on her including mine.

On her awaiting husband's face was overwhelming joy. He firmly grasped her arm as she stood next to him. Tears began to flow down the side of his face. Vows were exchanged and their lives intertwined. The scene held all of the poignancy of a storybook romance.

I can only imagine the day the Bride of Christ stands before her Bridegroom. All of the heavenly hosts will hush as this beautiful woman enters the great chamber. She will be a woman without equal; radiant and glorious. All of human history is rapidly racing toward a wedding ceremony.

Gazing upon our Bridegroom

"…come back, that we may gaze on you! Song of Solomon 6:13b

The Bride is now becoming more caught up in the piercing reality of Jesus, than what the world has to offer. We are being invited to participate in the greatest love affair time has ever known. It is a love that is higher than the loftiest mountains and deeper than the darkest sea. We are fortunate that the glorious bridegroom has remained true to His marriage proposal. The Song of Solomon conveys a wonderful picture of this passionate love.

> *"Place me like a seal over your heart, like a seal on your arm; for love is as strong as death, its jealousy unyielding as the grave. It burns like blazing fire, like a mighty flame. Many waters cannot quench love; rivers cannot wash it away. If one were to give all the wealth of his house for love, it would be utterly scorned." Song of Solomon 8:6-7*

In former days, the Bride could not raise her head and gaze upon the bridegroom. Sin and darkness weighed her down. Embarrassed and ashamed, the Bride was not worthy to enter the chamber of the King. In many

ways she felt like Israel during the time of Ezra. In
distress of his nation's condition, Ezra declared,

> *"O my God, I am too ashamed and disgraced to
> lift my face to you, my God, because our sins are
> higher than our heads and our guilt has reached
> to the heavens." Ezra 9:6*

Things have now changed. The bride is being
transformed in the glory of her bridegroom. The
darkest sins are being washed away by the blood of
Jesus. There is a renewed glory about her as innocence
is being restored. As the writer of Hebrews so
eloquently declared, *"...we have confidence to enter the
Most Holy Place by the blood of Jesus..." Hebrews 10:
19b.*

While anticipating a glorious wedding, the bride
is now learning to gaze upon her bridegroom.
She is learning that the majesty of her husband is
unsurpassed throughout time and eternity. She is
learning the truth the author Hebrews declared, *"Let us
fix our eyes on Jesus, the author and perfecter of our faith"
Hebrews 12:2a.* In the midst of her adoring gaze, the
glorious attributes of her bridegroom are uncovered.
She sees more clearly His innocence, love and justice.

God is innocent

"...God cannot be tempted by evil..." James 1:
13b

In the beginning, the serpent asked, *"Did God*
really say...?" Genesis 3:1b and since that moment
accusations have continued. Time and time again,
Satan has invited humanity to question the character
of God. When insurance companies refer to tornadoes,
earthquakes and floods as "acts of God", it is obvious
man blames the world's tragedies on the Lord.

Despite all of the horrible accusations, the innocence
of our Bridegroom reverberates throughout time. Peter
speaks of Jesus as a lamb "without blemish or defect"
1 Peter 1:19b. John declares even further that, *"...in*
Him is no sin." 1 John 3:5b. Ultimately the Prophet
Ezekiel records the disappointment of God as He
responds to the humiliation. *"They dishonored my holy*
name in the nations where they went...I am going to act,
but not for your sake. I will do something to help my holy
name." NCV Ezekiel 36:20a, 22b.

When first encountering the presence of God, my
husband was not shocked by wisdom, brilliance or
majesty. It was the piercing innocence that left him
gasping for air. Jesus possesses a child-likeness that is
absolutely untouched by evil. Void of all pretense, He
was not hiding anything, Jesus simply was - and in
Him Steve saw everything he ever wanted.

It is time to gaze upon the Bridegroom and declare like the Shulammite woman in Song of Solomon, *"All beautiful you are, my darling; there is no flaw in you" Song of Songs 4:7.* Our Lord and Savior, Jesus, is without fault. As you gaze upon Him, may you too find everything you ever wanted or needed.

God is Loving

> *"And so we know and rely on the love God has for us. God is love." 1 John 4:16*

Thomas Oden penned, *"The music God makes in creation is not a dirge, but a love song to, for and through creatures."*[18] God's love surpasses human knowledge and expresses itself throughout the generations. All of creation declares the wondrous love of God. Reflecting on the majesty of God's love, Paul wrote,

> *"Love is patient, love is kind. It does not envy, it does not boast, it is not proud. It is not rude, it is not self-seeking, it is not easily angered, it keeps no record of wrongs. Love does not delight in evil, but rejoices with the truth. It always protects, always trusts, always hopes, always perseveres." 1 Corinthians 13:4–7*

That passage is not alone. The reality of love resounds throughout scripture. The Apostle John affirmed that, *"…God so loved the World…" John 3:16a.* The God-kind of love values and cherishes. It gives of itself unconditionally. Later, the same apostle declared that,

"...Love is from God..." 1 John 4:7b. God is the only source of real love.

In response to the overwhelming love of God, Paul posed an important question, *"Who shall separate us from the love of Christ?" Romans 8:35.* I have learned that only we can separate ourselves from the love of God. A simple choice of whether or not we harden our hearts makes all the difference. In the midst of a world filled with hatred and scorn, the love of the bridegroom prevails.

Gaze upon His wondrous love and allow your heart to completely embrace it.

God is Just

> *"Righteousness and justice is the foundation of your throne; Mercy and truth go before Your face." Psalm 89:14*

Our gracious Bridegroom is also righteous. As one of prophets declared, *"Your eyes are too pure to behold evil, and you cannot look on wrongdoing." Habbakuk 1: 12-13.* Many other passages depict God as a righteous judge. In the Torah, Abraham affirms, *"Shall not the Judge of all the earth do what is just?" Genesis 18: 25.* Later the Apostle John affirms, *"With justice he judges and makes war. His eyes are like a blazing fire" Revelation 19:11b -12a.* Scriptures continually affirm that God despises injustice and rights the wrongs.

Drawing a false dichotomy, the justice of God is sometimes pitted against the love of God. I recently heard somebody say, *"How could a loving God, send someone to Hell?"* It is forgotten that God is both holy and loving at the same time. He loves in justice and judges in love. This truth is perfectly clarified in the work of the Cross. On Calvary, justice and love met together in perfect harmony. As the Psalmist declared, *"Love and faithfulness meet together; righteousness and peace kiss each other." Psalm 85:10.* When Jesus appears, his eyes will be blazing with fire. The loving bridegroom will be revealed in the strength of a righteousness judge.

Gaze upon the glorious justice of our great King.

We Shall Be Like Him

"When He is revealed, we shall be like Him." 1 John 3:2

The Bible makes it clear, Jesus will not be returning for an ugly bride. The Bride of Christ will be a beautiful reflection of her Bridegroom's innocence. She will be clothed in justice and in love. Walking in His glory, wrinkles and unkempt hair will be no more. Indiscretion is a thing of the past. Her flowing white dress will shimmer in the glory of holiness. Her radiant face will reflect her passion for her bridegroom. The Apostle Paul writes,

*"Christ loved the church and gave himself up
for her to make her holy, cleansing her by the
washing with water through the word, and
to present her to himself as a radiant church,
without stain or wrinkle or any other blemish,
but holy and blameless." Ephesians 5:25b-27*

The time is coming when the Bride will have
completed all her ceremonial washings and beauty
treatments. The time will come when the Bridegroom
presents her to Himself. The earthly "veil" will be
lifted back from her face. What a time of rejoicing.

But what will this glorious woman look like?

When our bridegroom appears, we will be like him.
John declares, *"We know that when He appears we shall
be like Him, for we shall see Him as He is" 1 John 3:
2* Imagine the splendor of seeing Jesus as He truly is.
No more veils. No more seeing through a glass darkly.
Imagine the innocent eyes of the bridegroom looking
into the face of His beloved. The Word declares that
she *"...will receive the crown of life that God promised to
those who loved Him." James 1:12*

Astonishingly the Bride is a reflection of the
Bridegroom!

Return to the Beginning

Then the angel showed me the river of the waters of life, as clear as crystal, flowing from the throne of God and of the Lamb down the middle of the great street of the city. On each side of the river stood the tree of life, bearing twelve crops of fruit, yielding its fruit every month. And the leaves of the tree are for the healing of the nations. No longer will there be any curse. The throne of God and of the Lamb will be in the city, and his servants will serve him. They will see his face, and his name will be on their foreheads. Revelation 22:2-4

As the final curtain descends and our story comes full circle, we find that God is bringing us back to the beginning. Passing through the shadows of time, we once more find ourselves standing before the Tree of Life. Only this time everything has changed. The bitter curse is gone and innocence has been restored.

*   No longer shall we have to hide

    And the leaves of the tree are for the healing of the nations. Revelation 22:2b

*   No longer shall we betray

    "...the Lamb will be in the city, and his servants will serve him." Revelation 22:3b

*   No Longer shall we be barren

*"…bearing twelve crops of fruit, yielding its
fruit every month. Revelation 22:2b*

- No Longer shall we be Banished

   *They will see his face, and his name will be on
   their foreheads. Revelation 22:4b*

Jesus, the "Last Adam" is coming back for the "Last
Eve," an innocent, child-like bride. She will look into
his eyes and say, "I do!" and they will serve each other
for eternity.

Application Questions

- What becomes the obsession of the future Bride as she awaits her Bridegroom?

- What does the bride discover about the Bridegroom as she gazes upon Him?

- Explain the concept, "God loves in justice and judges in love."

- How does the innocence of our Bridegroom impact your life?

- What efforts are you making to be found spotless, blameless and at peace with Him?

- How has the last Eve come full circle?

- When we reign with the bridegroom, for what purpose will the "leaves of the tree" be?

- What four conditions no longer describe the Bride when she is united with her Bridegroom?

  Lord Jesus, I desire You as never before. How I long for the veil to be removed that I might see you clearly! My greatest passion is to see your face. I am absolutely devoted to you forever!

Postscript

I sincerely pray truths discussed in this book have stirred your heart. Like salt, I hope the concepts have brought a thirst for intimacy with our great bridegroom, Jesus. It is my prayer that you are experiencing a hunger so intense that you will take action.

As profound as the concepts are in this book, reading is just a beginning. I want to remind you that my own life changed when I took action. My innocence had been stolen by a life-long "bitter root." My breakthrough began after I acknowledged the truth and stopped justifying myself. I humbly submitted to the Lord and that bitter root was violently uprooted. Innocence was restored! I want to encourage you to take action. Submit to the power of the Holy Spirit and find the freedom to pursue your destiny.

This is the day and this is the hour! It is time for you to break free from all the things that inhibit you. Grab a hold of the power of God and allow Him to usher in all that He has designed for your life. Impossibilities become powerful realities in the glory of His presence. In this hour we cannot survive unless we are bathed in His glory.

Oh how I wish you would visit our church! Come witness a people who are enjoying the restoration of innocence. As our congregation comes together, we have the privilege of welcoming the presence of the King of Kings. Again and again, He graces us by opening the windows of heaven. Sometimes our hearts explode with joy, while on other occasions our bodies collapse under the weight of His glory. There are moments when conviction floods our souls and there are other times when our spirits soar. It doesn't matter what God chooses to do in our services, His presence is our very life.

A critical decision lies at the crossroads of our lives. Shall we chose, indifference or the heart of the Bridegroom? Will we become a people of whom it is said, *"They overcame him(the accuser) by the blood of the Lamb and by the word of their testimony; they did not love their lives so much as to shrink from death" Revelation 12:11*? May our response be a resounding "Yes!"

> *"Lord Jesus, breathe the breath of life into my nostrils! May your Spirit break through every "wall" until my life is wholly exposed. Gift me with courage and perseverance. Don't let me rest until innocence is restored in my life. Let me live as a radiant Bride who only loves the magnificent King of Kings."*

Sources

[1] Pelham Gross; *Cornfield Revival: An Experiential Account;* Unedited and unpublished Manuscript; September 1998; Smithton, Missouri.

[2] Student; *Assessment of Revival Services;* Dr. David Nichol's Class; North Central Bible College; Minneapolis, Minnesota; 1998.

[3] W.T. Stead; "The Story of the Awakening"; *The Story of the Welsh Revival;* Revell Publishing; New York, New York; Copyright © 1905.

[4] Randy Lohman; *Personal Journal;* February, 1996.

[5] Randy Lohman; Testimony; Christian Life Fellowship; Monee, Illinois; January 2, 1999.

[6] Emily Lohman; *Personal Reflections;* February, 2000.

[7] Charles A. Johnson; *The Frontier Campmeeting;* Pages 64-65; Southern Methodist University Press; Dallas, Texas; Copyright © 1955.

[8] Maria Woodworth-Etter; *Diary of Signs and Wonders;* Harrison House Publishers; P.O. Box 35035, Tulsa Oklahoma; © Copyright 1916.

[9] Maria Woodworth-Etter; *Diary of Signs and Wonders;* Harrison House Publishers; P.O. Box 35035, Tulsa Oklahoma; © Copyright 1916.

[10] Aimee Semple-Mcpherson; *The Story of My Life;* Echo Park Evangelistic Association; Los Angeles, California; © Copyright 1951.

[11] Aimee Semple-Mcpherson; *The Story of My Life;* Echo Park Evangelistic Association; Los Angeles, California; © Copyright 1951.

[12] Kuhlman, Kathryn; *God Can Do It Again;* Bridge Publishing Inc.; 2500 Hamilton Blvd., South Plainfield, NJ 07080; © 1969.

[13] David J. Williams; *Paul's Metaphors: Their Context and Character;* P.54; Hendrickson Publishers; P.O. Box 3473, Peabody, Massachusetts 01961-3473; Copyright © 1999.

[14] Steve Hill; *Hot From the Preacher's Mound, Second Inning;* Pages 10 – 11; Together in the Harvest Publications; P.O. Box 2090; Foley, Alabama 36536; Copyright © 1998.

[15]Leonard Ravenhill; Why Revival Tarries; Page 49; Bethany Publishers; 6820 Auto Club Road; Minneapolis, Minnesota 55438; Copyright © 1959.

[16]Hannah Whitall Smith; *The Unselfishness of God: My Spiritual Autobiography*; Littlebrook Publishing, Inc.; Princeton, New Jersey 08540; Copyright © 1987.

[17]Ruth Ward Heflin; *Revival Glory*; McDougal Publishing; P.O. Box 3595, Hagerstown, MD 21742-3595; Copyright © 1998

[18]Thomas C. Oden; *The Living God: Systematic Theology Volume One*; Page 118; Prince Press; P.O. Box 3473 Peabody, MA 01961-3473 Copyright © 2001.

Kathy Gray is available for speaking engagements.

For additional information about the ministry of
Kathy Gray, contact:

World Revival Church
9900 View High Drive
Kansas City, MO 64134
Phone: 1-877-804-LIFE
E-mail: wrc@wrckc.com
Website: www.worldrevivalchurch.com

Join the World Revival Network

The World Revival Network of Ministries gathers and equips like-minded pastors, leaders and ministry minded people for Spirit-led ministry and fellowship. The Network is a place for ministry-minded people to exchange ideas, develop edifying relationships and become a part of a united voice that promotes the message and model of revival throughout the world.

Post Office Box 11678
Kansas City, MO 64138
Phone: 1-877-804-LIFE
E-mail: wrn@wrckc.com
Website: www.worldrevivalnetwork.com

Preparing Leaders with the

Fire of Revival

and the Word of the Kingdom

9900 View High Drive

Kansas City, MO 64134

Phone: 1-877-804-LIFE

E-mail: sdgray@wrckc.com

Website: www.worldrevivalschool.com